Chinese Internal Boxing

CHINESE INTERNAL BOXING

Techniques of Hsing-i & Pa-kua

Robert W. Smith
and Allen Pittman

TUTTLE PUBLISHING
Tokyo · Rutland, Vermont · Singapore

Please note that the publisher and authors of this instructional book are NOT RESPONSIBLE in any manner whatsoever for any injury that may result from practicing the techniques and/or following the instructions given within. Martial arts training can be dangerous—both to you and to others—if not practiced safely. If you're in doubt as to how to proceed or whether your practice is safe, consult with a trained martial arts teacher before beginning. Since the physical activities described herein may be too strenuous in nature for some readers, it is also essential that a physician be consulted prior to training.

Published by Tuttle Publishing, an imprint of Periplus Editions (HK) Ltd., with editorial offices at 364 Innovation Drive, North Clarendon, Vermont 05759 U.S.A.

Library of Congress Cataloging-in-Publication Data
Smith, Robert W., 1926–
Chinese internal boxing : techniques of hsing-i & pa kua / Robert Smith, Allen Pittman.
    p. cm.
Includes index.
ISBN 0-8048-3824-0
1. Hand-to-hand fighting, Oriental-Psychological aspects. 2. Tai chi. 3. Kung fu. I. Pittman, Allen. II. Title.
GV1112.S58 2006
796.815'5—dc22

                         2006040392

ISBN-10: 0-8048-3824-0
ISBN-13: 978-0-8048-3824-5

Distributed by:
**North America, Latin America
& Europe**
364 Innovation Drive
North Clarendon, VT 05759-9436 U.S.A.
Tel: 1 (802) 773-8930
Fax: 1 (802) 773-6993
info@tuttlepublishing.com
www.tuttlepublishing.com

Asia Pacific
Berkeley Books Pte. Ltd.
130 Joo Seng Road #06-01
Singapore 368357
Tel: (65) 6280-1330
Fax: (65) 6280-6290
inquiries@periplus.com.sg
www.periplus.com

First edition
10 09 08 07 06   10 9 8 7 6 5 4 3 2 1

Printed in the United States of America

TUTTLE PUBLISHING ® is a registered trademark of Tuttle Publishing, a division of Periplus Editions (HK) Ltd.

Contents

Preface

We wrote this book believing that there are many people who are interested in the Chinese internal martial arts of Hsing-i (pronounced "shing-ee") and Pa-kua (pronounced "ba-gwa") as they were traditionally taught on the mainland.* Such people understand that these arts are meditative forms of health and body management from which self defense spills over, rather than an aggressive combat form, of which the world already has too many. As a system of self defense, however, it is harshly effective.

Besides training for several years in Taiwan under the Hsing-i and Pa-kua masters Hung I-hsiang and his brother Hung I-mien, Mr. Smith was also fortunate enough to be allowed to study under Wang Shu-chin, Kuo Feng-ch'ih, Yuan Tao, and other masters. His training path is very clearly outlined in his *Chinese Boxing: Masters and Methods* (Tokyo, 1974) and other books. Some twenty years later, Mr. Pittman, one of Mr. Smith's senior students, went to Taiwan seeking the old masters, but found that many had died. In Taipei, however, he came across a still hardy Hung I-mien,

---

* In this book, Chinese terms are transliterated with the Wade-Giles system, except where the word is already widely used with a different spelling, as, for instance, "Peking," "Nanking," etc.

who invited him to share his home as a live-in student. After absorbing Hung's Hsing-i and Pa-kua, he traveled south to Taichung to practice with the sons of the late Ch'en P'an-ling—Yuan-ch'ao and Yun-ch'ing—and the senior students of the late Wang Shu-chin.

From these experiences, the basic forms of these two master teachers as taught to the authors were assimilated and consolidated. This is the first time that they have been taught to the West in such minute detail. We hope that Western students will benefit from this clear exposition of teachings that were once only passed on to initiates deemed worthy of learning the styles and being entrusted with their transmission.

The Hsing-i forms in this book are generally those of Ch'en P'an-ling as elaborated in his *Chung-hua kuo-shu chiao-ts'ai ch'uan-chi* [The Complete Instructional Guide to Chinese Martial Arts] (Taipei, 1978). The Pa-kua forms given in this book are essentially those of Wang Shu-chin as elaborated in his *Pa-kua lien-huan chang* [Pa-kua Linked Palm] (Taipei, 1978; privately published). Also used as sources were the two books considered to be the best ever written on the art: Sun Lu-tang's classic *Pa-kua ch'uan hsueh* [A Study of Pa-kua Boxing] (Peking, 1916) and Huang Po-nien's *Lung-hsing pa-kua chang* [Dragon-Style Pa-kua Palm] (Shanghai, 1936). These are the orthodox, traditional methods long practiced on the mainland and in Taiwan—the authentic forms from which most other versions derive. They are being published here so that students can learn the *real* forms as opposed to the Americanized offshoots. These forms are designed to refine your nature, reform your temperament, and return you to your original self.

But it is a rash reader who thinks that by simply buying this book, he or she will mysteriously be enabled to absorb the teachings it contains. To learn any of the three internal arts—Tai-chi, Hsing-i, or Pa-kua—requires commitment, not mere involvement. Being involved or committed is like ham and eggs: the chicken is involved but the pig is committed! This is not a coffee-table book—it should be sweat over and on. We have labored over its presentation, carefully blending the pictorial with the textual, so that the student can learn without going astray. But our efforts are in vain if the student does not practice. He or she must practice assiduously for a long time—"The years see what the day will never know"—if progress is to come. Confucius once said that if he gave a student one corner of a handkerchief, it was up to the student to find the other three corners. This book is but one corner; your practice will help you find the other three.

Acknowledgments

The writing of this book was eased by the help and support of several friends and colleagues: John Lang, who diligently worked at every level of its preparation; James Klebau, a true professional, who caught the inner spirit of the forms in his fine photographs; Pat Kenny, who helped with the graphics; Bob Arief, Al Carson, Jay Falleson, Steve Goodson, and Irene Pittman, who proofread and corrected the manuscript; Y. W. Chang, Ann Carruthers, Pat McGowan, Chris Bates, Richard Cress, Danny Emerick, and Ben Lo, who acted as sounding-boards; Anne Pavay and Alice Smith, who patiently typed the manuscript; Stephen Comee, who studies under Wang Shu-chin's successor and who worked hard as the editor and designer of this book; the Charles E. Tuttle Company, which agreed to publish this book; and all the masters and teachers of the Chinese internal martial arts who have given their time and instruction—without their generosity we would never have been able to study these arts. To all of these and to others who helped bring this project to fruition, the authors gratefully bow in deep thanks.

Robert W. Smith
Allen Pittman
Flat Rock, NC

PART ONE	Introduction to Hsing-i Boxing

The theory of Hsing-i is simple. The aim is to divest ourselves of what we acquire after birth and return to the origin (the oneness) through the Five Fists and the Twelve Animal Styles. All of these derive from one style. Keeping the mind calm and at the tan-t'ien *(below the navel), we will come to the one.*

—Master Liu Hsiao-lan

1
What Is Hsing-i?

NAME AND THING

The name of this style of Chinese boxing, *hsing-i ch'uan,* literally means "the kind of boxing *(ch'uan)* in which the forms *(hsing)* are created by the mind *(i).*" In this "mind-formed fist," the mind predominates over mere physicality and, harmoniously blending thought and action, expresses itself in moving forms and postures dating back some 400 years.

Hsing-i is one of the three traditional Chinese forms of internal boxing, the other two being T'ai-chi ("tie-jee") and Pa-kua ("bah-gwah").[1] Each of the three internal arts is a distinct style of boxing, yet each shares with the others the fact that it is essentially a form of moving meditation. Boxing is something of a misnomer. Each of the internal arts is actually a self-contained and complete system of exercise that is permeated with functions combining grappling and striking, and that, through correct practice, is seen to be a superior system of self-defense. Each of them, through diligent practice, becomes a part of your life. Self-improvement on all levels—physical, emotional, men-

---

[1]   These internal fighting systems differ from the Shaolin and other external traditions in that they depend upon the practitioner's ability to cultivate and use *ch'i* rather than only outer muscular strength. Internal masters develop and use the sinews, ligaments, and tendons, whereas external masters concentrate on the larger outer musculature.

tal, and spiritual—is the reason we train in an art: it is there if needed, but it is used only in the greatest extremity because of its inherent power. In a utilitarian society, this might seem a silly motivation—to learn something so that you will never have to use it. But Hsing-i is an internal art, and, as such, it is more concerned with life, health, and creativity than with death, competition, or destruction.

Indeed, none of the internal arts has free sparring, which is a type of competitive fighting and which is avoided in learning the internal arts. Rather, we box mainly with ourselves, and by learning the skill there is no need to contest it. George Mallory, who died on Mount Everest in 1924, once explained why men climbed mountains (''Because they are there'') by asking, ''Whom have we conquered?'' and answering, ''None but ourselves.'' Internal boxing is essentially a method of transforming the self. The traditional Doctrine of Three Layers (*San-ts'eng t'ao-li*) discusses this process of change in terms of Taoist philosophy, wherein it is thought that one's original state (*hsu,* or emptiness) is filled by a seed-essence (*ching*) at birth, and that this life essence is so transformed into intrinsic energy (*ch'i*) and further into vital spirit (*shen*) through practice that one returns to the original state of emptiness (*hsu*). It advises the student to change essence into *ch'i,* *ch'i* into spirit, and then to restore to spirit the original emptiness. Put simply, the boxing is at once the tool and the product of this creative process. Because it is creative, it cannot lead to destruction. True enough, the old masters met challenges. But more often than not they sent the challenger away a friend—happy because he had been soundly defeated, educated but not seriously hurt.

The most famous such match reportedly occurred in Peking between Kuo Yun-shen, the famed Hsing-i adept known as ''the Divine Crushing Fist,'' and Tung Hai-ch'uan, the modern father of Pa-kua. Kuo tried unsuccessfully for two days to dent Tung's defense and on the third day was completely defeated by the Pa-kua master. The two

2. The "Crushing Fist" of Hsing-i, Peking, ca. 1930

became lifelong friends; indeed, so impressed were they with the art of the other that they signed a pact requiring students of each discipline to cross-train in the other. Thus, to this day, the systems are coupled, complementary, and taught together. In fact, the principles cited for Hsing-i in this book are equally applicable to Pa-kua.

Done correctly, Hsing-i strikes are extremely dangerous. That is why there is no sparring: if the punches are pulled or muted in any way, they are not Hsing-i. Thus, Western boxing and karate cannot help the Hsing-i boxer to sharpen his skills. In this respect, Hsing-i is similar to the ancient forms of some Japanese martial arts, which have remained the same over the centuries because of their difficulty and intrinsically dangerous natures. If regulated, restricted, and made sportive, such arts, including Hsing-i and Pa-kua, lose their essence.

Hsing-i nonetheless proved its worth in regulated Chinese national boxing tournaments: its exponents led the winners of the tournaments held in Nanking (1928), Shanghai (1929), Hangchou (1929), and again in Nanking (1933). The most successful provincial competitions were conducted in Honan province by Ch'en P'an-ling, whose method we teach here.

Being a form of meditation, Hsing-i requires strong dedication to regular practice in a quiet place (Fig. 2). You must create for yourself

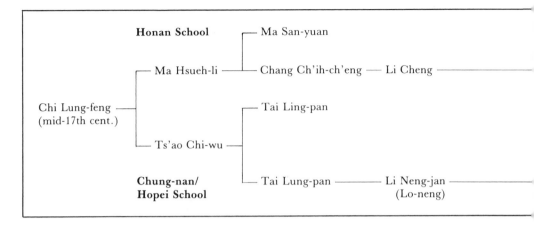

Table 1. Abbreviated Hsing-i Lineage

a routine based on a quiet attentiveness, which may at first bore you. Ultimate skill comes from this quiet as much as from the physiological and psychological aspects of the exercise itself. When the silence releases its energy, a quiet mind is produced and your whole being becomes more active.

A system relying totally on body mechanics remains at the level of calisthenics and rudimentary fighting, Hsing-i trains the mind even more than it does the body. The mind *wills* and the body *responds*. There is a kind of reciprocity at work, for as the body is exercised dynamically and internally it returns health benefits to both itself and the mind. And the process continues, the mind being the master.

Springing from Taoist and Buddhist techniques, Hsing-i is cooperative, not competitive; it emphasizes *being* and *becoming* rather than *thinking* and *doing*. But it requires discipline and much hard work. Because Hsing-i gets little media reinforcement, you must motivate and sustain yourself. Progress will be slower than in the external arts, but since the skill you achieve comes from your mind and your internal organs, it will be deeper and will last longer.

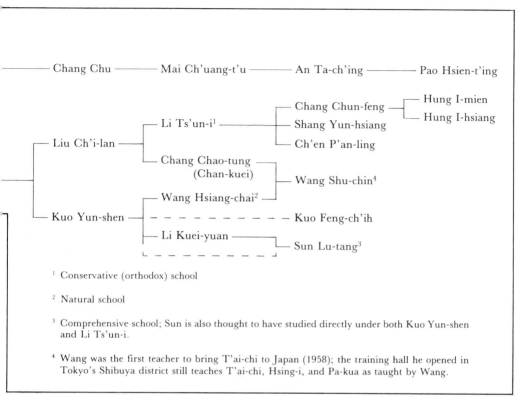

Chang Chu ——— Mai Ch'uang-t'u ——— An Ta-ch'ing ——— Pao Hsien-t'ing

Liu Ch'i-lan
  — Li Ts'un-i[1] ———
    — Chang Chun-feng —
      — Hung I-mien
      — Hung I-hsiang
    — Shang Yun-hsiang
    — Ch'en P'an-ling
  — Chang Chao-tung (Chan-kuei) —
    — Wang Shu-chin[4]
  — Wang Hsiang-chai[2] —

Kuo Yun-shen
  — — — — — — — — — — Kuo Feng-ch'ih
  — Li Kuei-yuan ———
    — Sun Lu-tang[3]

[1] Conservative (orthodox) school

[2] Natural school

[3] Comprehensive school; Sun is also thought to have studied directly under both Kuo Yun-shen and Li Ts'un-i.

[4] Wang was the first teacher to bring T'ai-chi to Japan (1958); the training hall he opened in Tokyo's Shibuya district still teaches T'ai-chi, Hsing-i, and Pa-kua as taught by Wang.

HISTORY AND MASTERS

Traditionally, it is taught that Hsing-i was created by a general of the Northern Sung dynasty (960–1127) named Yueh Fei; and some even credit its genesis to Bodhidharma, the monk who brought Zen from India to China in the sixth century—neither of these claims can be substantiated. Both are the stuff of legend.

What is known with certainty is that a man named Chi Lung-feng is the earliest recorded father of the art, but we know very little about him save that he was from Shanghai, excelled in spear-play, and learned Hsing-i in the Chung-nan mountains of Shansi province between 1637 and 1662 from a Taoist hermit. Chi's top two students, Ts'ao

Chi-wu of Shansi and Ma Hsueh-li of Honan, spread the art to others through whom the teachings have come down to the present in two lines of unbroken succession. Honan, Hopei, and Shansi supplied most of the great teachers, among whom were: Li Neng-jan, Sung Shih-jung, Chang Chih-ch'eng, Ch'e I-chai, Kuo Yun-shen, Li Cheng, Li Ts'un-i, Shang Yun-hsiang, Wang Hsiang-chai, Sun Lu-t'ang, Ch'en P'an-ling, Chang Chun-feng, and Wang Shu-chin (Table 1). Ch'en P'an-ling studied the orthodox Hsing-i system taught in this book directly from the great Li Ts'un-i.

2

Theories Behind the Art

BREATHING AND BODY

Correct breathing uses the diaphragm, a large muscle that stretches from the lumbar spine to the rib cage, separating the heart-lung area from the digestive organs. Abdominal breathing articulates the intercostal muscles and ribs and efficiently positions the shoulder blades and clavicles, thus assisting coordination of the upper torso and supporting the head and arms. All movements are coordinated with the breathing, achieving, as master Sung Shih-jung wrote, "full calmness, full regulation of breathing, and full coordination of the body." Initially, breathe naturally without thinking of inhalation and exhalation. Breathe only through your nostrils, filling your belly. Keep your tongue on the roof of your mouth, your lips relaxed. Later, pay attention to your inhalation, sinking the *ch'i* (intrinsic energy) to your *tan-t'ien* (the psychic center just below the navel). Specifically, when practicing the forms, you should exhale through the nostrils as you apply the movement, but simultaneously, sink a part of the breath down to the *tan-t'ien*. If you reach the top level of the art, you will not be conscious of breathing. As master Kuo Yun-shen wrote: "There is no sound, no smell, and everything is empty."

Hsing-i enlivens your muscles by expansion and contraction, strengthens the ligaments and tendons, eases the circulation of both the blood and *ch'i,* and produces rapid, effortless movement. The muscles and sinews are made more elastic and lively while being strengthened in a process similar to that of the refining of raw iron into steel. Open your body: become familiar with the pull of gravity and with a precise, straight posture. Relax your shoulders: become aware of the position of the shoulder blades. Bend your legs: become aware of the way you hold the pelvis. Hold your neck straight: keep the head erect, as though it were being pulled up with a string, and look directly ahead. Relax your buttocks, holding the sacrum naturally straight.

These training principles bearing on the muscles are important, but if you pay attention only to the external musculature, the blood and *ch'i* will not be able to circulate freely—and *ch'i* is the foundation of the art. It must be sunk to the *tan-t'ien,* whence it circulates throughout the body. The ancients said that the original *ch'i* (*yuan ch'i*)—"the power that keeps the sky blue and the earth calm and also makes for achievement in man"—must be maintained. Besides cultivating your *ch'i,* you must also rid yourself of bad habits and thoughts, calm your heart, and thus attain sincerity.

Hsing-i gives good health and makes your body strong. Your internal organs are like the engine parts of a car, your muscles like its outer surface. Blood and *ch'i* are the fuel generating movement. If the engine parts are broken, the car will not run, even if it is full of gasoline and looks fine. Therefore, priority is given to the internal organs, which leads to a natural cultivation of *ch'i,* rather than to the outer muscles.

Coming from stillness, the upright postures teach grounding by lowering the waist and pelvis, relaxing the buttocks, and bending the legs. The rhythm of the movements provides aerobic benefits, while the alternate training of moving and pausing assists the sense of timing and rooting. *Natural* coordination is "restored" through movements stressing opposite-hand-and-foot substantiality as well as synchronized same-hand-and-foot movements. Finally, because balance is lost when you place your weight 50-50 between your legs ("double weighting"),

Hsing-i depends upon single-weighted, "one-legged" boxing that allows you to distinguish the empty (*yin*) and the full (*yang*) and that enhances freer movement.

EXERCISE AND MEDITATION

Like Pa-kua, Hsing-i derives from ancient Buddhist and especially Taoist meditation practices. The physiological and esoteric principles have been explicated by master Kuo Yun-shen, and what follows in this section is a summary of his teachings. Taoist meditation and internal boxing both have the goal of emptiness. But where meditation goes from inaction to action, boxing goes in the opposite direction, from action to inaction. From the Taoists, the Hsing-i masters borrowed the following concept of changes:

Hsing-i Stages	Taoist Sedentary Changes	Body Changes	Type of Energy
1. Change essence to *ch'i*	Hard burning	Bones	Visible
2. Change *ch'i* to spirit	Summoning fire	Sinews	Concealed
3. Change spirit to emptiness	Divine fire	Marrow	Mysterious

To get visible energy, you must be centered and balanced. This energy transforms essence (actually connoting but meaning much more than just sexual energy) into *ch'i,* which changes the bones. When you stand and move, your bones become hard and your body becomes solid like a mountain. After rigorous practice for an extended period, your dispersed *ch'i* is concentrated at your navel and all parts of your body become coordinated.

The next stage is concealed energy. Developing from the first stage, it is free, relaxed, and natural. It is not soft like snow, but elastic like grass. Here, *ch'i* is transformed into vital spirit and the sinews are energized.

In the next and highest stage, that of mysterious energy, the bone marrow is washed and cleaned, relaxation is complete, and your internal organs are so purified that you become as light as a feather. The energy becomes so concentrated that its nature is restored to that of original emptiness. Your actions are the same, but your energy remains inside, controlled by the mind.

But how does Hsing-i manifest itself in these three stages? Traditionally, it is described thus: in the visible stage, it is "like a steel chisel that thrusts out strongly and falls lightly like a piece of bamboo"; in the concealed stage, it "starts like an arrow and falls weightlessly, like the wind"; and in the highest stage, it "follows the wind and chases the moon." An outsider never sees it hit. Here, the mind is mindless; you do nothing and have done everything. In the emptiness you find your pre-birth energy, but if you search too hard it will elude you. It is better to think that you already possess such energy. This will influence your mind, the embodiment of all actions. Remember—Hsing-i is boxing with the mind.

PART TWO

Hsing-i Training

3

The Basics

All Hsing-i movements are performed lightly and briskly, and the entire body is relaxed, without the strong muscular contraction of karate and other external forms. To learn to do Hsing-i properly, you must first master the following fundamentals.

THE FIVE POSITIONS

Chicken Leg	One leg supports the body while the other is held off the ground.
Dragon Body	The body stands in three straight sections: heels to knees, knees to hips, and hips to head.
Bear Shoulders	The shoulders are rounded, curving from the spine like a bow.
Eagle Claws	The fingers clutch tightly like talons.
Tiger Embrace	The arms menace threateningly, looking like a tiger leaving its den.

THE SIX COORDINATIONS

The six coordinations are extremely important to the correct practice of Hsing-i, since, if the *ch'i* and the movement are not coordinated, then the posture will be incorrect and you will not be able to use your *ch'i*. If the body is straight and does not lean in any direction, the mind will be clear, the *ch'i* will be harmonious, and the movement will be natural. Thus, internally, the spirit controls the mind, which controls the *ch'i*, which controls the strength. Externally, the hands pressing downward correlate with the heels turning outward; the sinking of the elbows is correlated with the slight inward pressing of the knees; and the shoulders and thighs relax. Total *true* movement can come about only if these six coordinations are unified, harmonized, and maintained.

Internal	External
Spirit — Mind	Shoulders — Thighs
Mind — *Ch'i*	Elbows — Knees
Ch'i — Strength	Hands — Feet

THE NINE WORDS

1) Press your head upward, your tongue forward and upward (so that it touches the upper palate), and your palms strongly to the front.

2) When you "button down" your shoulders, the chest empties and *ch'i* flows freely to the elbows. When you "button down" your hands and feet, the palms and soles empty and *ch'i* flows freely to them. When your teeth "button down," your tendons and bones contract.

3) By rounding your back, your strength "urges" the body, your coccyx straightens, and your spirit rises. By rounding the chest, the elbows protect the heart and the breath (*ch'i*) moves freely. By rounding the tiger's mouth (*hu k'ou*, the space be-

tween the thumb and index finger), your energy (*ching*) is directed outward and your arms develop ''embracing'' energy.

4) Learn to keep your mind (heart: *hsin*) relaxed so that it can respond to any situation, to keep your eyes alert, and to keep your hands ahead of your enemy (i.e., to move them in such a way that the enemy cannot see them strike).

5) Hold your *ch'i* securely within your *tan-t'ien*; hold your upper breath gently so that fear has no place in which to take hold; and hold your ribs safely within the elbows, so that there is no way for danger to approach them.

6) When you sink your *ch'i* down into your *tan-t'ien*, you will become as stable as a mountain. When you sink your shoulders, your arms will spring to life, ''urged'' on by the elbows. When you sink your arms, they naturally protect the ribs.

7) When you bend your arms, strength will be abundant. When you bend your knees, you will be rooted to the earth with strength. When you cup your palms, strength will concentrate in them. When you bend or curve these parts of the body, they naturally contract and expand, thus unblocking the flow of energy.

8) When you straighten your neck, your head will become erect, as though floating in the air, and your *ch'i* will rise up strongly. When you straighten your spine, your strength will reach the four extremities (the top of the head, the hands, the knees, and the feet) and *ch'i* will fill the whole body. When you straighten your knees, the flow of your *ch'i* will be calm and your spirit will be harmonious, making you like a tree sending roots down deep into the earth, from which it absorbs energy.

9) Hold you arms so that they embrace the chest, protecting your

3–7. The Basic Motions: 3) Starting Position; 4) Rise; 5) Drill;

heart and ready to strike out like a tiger lunging at its prey. Keep your *ch'i* down so that it embraces the *tan-t'ien*, allowing the *ch'i* to flow freely throughout the body. Let your courage rise up and embrace the body; this will let your *ch'i* flow so freely that it covers the body with a mantle of protection.

OTHER POINTERS

Some other pointers that should be kept in mind when practicing are:
1) The tip of your nose, your fingertips, and the tips of your toes should be kept on one imaginary line.
2) Your body should fall as your *ch'i* rises, and should rise as your *ch'i* falls.
3) Your hands should rise like iron spades and fall like scythes.
4) When you use but one hand, it should thrust out like a hawk raiding a forest and fall like a swallow sweeping over the surface of a lake. When you use both hands, they should rise up like a tiger leaping out of its lair and fall like a sledgehammer breaking bricks.
5) The fundamental tactic—and one that the old masters practiced by the hour—is the same as in Pa-kua: rise, drill, fall, and overturn (Figs. 3–7). Each part must be clearly differentiated; all must be done like lightning. This is eased by keeping your body relaxed until the final instant. The tactic can be

6) Fall; and 7) Overturn

used—either quickly or slowly—in all directions to close up the distance between you and your opponent.

6) Summarizing, your

        waist — sinks

        shoulders — shrink

        chest — withdraws

        head — pushes up

        tongue — touches the roof of the mouth

        hands — feel as if pushing upward

        sacrum — circles inward and upward

4

Practicing the Five Fists

H sing-i's five basic forms are also called the five elements (*wu hsing*), after the five essential elements of traditional Chinese cosmology—metal, water, wood, fire, and earth. Each of these elements is capable of generating or destroying another element, as shown in the diagram below. The lines forming the pentagon indicate generation, while those forming the star indicate destruction.

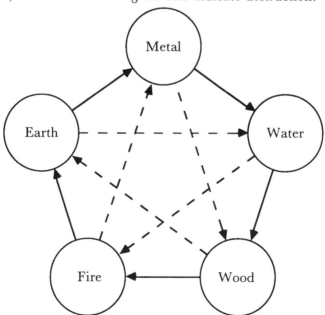

The FIVE FISTS were originally arranged in the same sequence as the order of generation of elements from metal to earth, and some schools of the orthodox Chung-nan line, such as Wang Shu-chin's, still follow that order, each fist symbolizing an element that generates the next one. Sun Lu-t'ang, Yuan Tao, Chen P'an-ling, and others in the orthodox school, however, reversed the order of water and wood, placing CRUSHING before DRILLING (Table 2). Thus, that is the sequence we have presented here.

The FIVE FISTS are as natural as a baby's movements. But because they are natural, they are difficult for people in a tense world to learn, and, after long practice, they can be dangerous if not controlled. They are correlated with the five elements, the organs of the body, and the flow of *ch'i* as follows:

Table 2.   The Five Correspondences

Fist	Element	Organs	Action of *Ch'i*
1. SPLITTING (*p'i-ch'uan*)	Metal	Lungs, Large Intestine	Rises and falls like an axe
2. CRUSHING (*peng-ch'uan*)	Wood	Liver, Gall bladder	Expands and contracts simultaneously
3. DRILLING (*tsuan-ch'uan*)	Water	Kidneys, Bladder	Flows in curving eddies or shoots like lightning
4. POUNDING (*p'ao-ch'uan*)	Fire	Heart, Pericardium	Fires suddenly like a projectile from a gun
5. CROSSING (*heng-ch'uan*)	Earth	Spleen, Stomach	Strikes forward with rounded energy

8

PREPARATION

The static INFINITY POSTURE (*wu chi*), a balance between suspension and rootedness, is the basis for Hsing-i movement. Your feet are at 45°, left foot facing front and heels touching, with the legs straight but with the knees slightly bent, and the pelvis is held in a natural position. Your head is suspended, allowing your spine to straighten. Relaxed shoulders that hang naturally in line with your hips allow the weight of your upper body to fall directly over your pelvic girdle and into your legs, creating the sense of "suspended by the crown of the head and rooted in the feet." Your mind and *ch'i* are centered in the *tan-t'ien* (Fig. 8).

9   10   11

BEGINNING

Stand in the INFINITY POSTURE and raise both arms out to the sides, palms down, twisting your torso slightly rightward (Fig. 9). Take your hands past your shoulders overhead, shoulder width apart, palms still down (Fig. 10). Continuing with your torso turned to the right, keep your knees together and sink your body as you lower your palms down the front of your body and close them into fists, while shifting most of your weight onto your right foot (Fig. 11).

Turn your waist leftward, DRILLING your right fist upward and forward (Fig. 12), palm up, to eyebrow level. Simultaneously, withdraw your left fist, palm down, to your left hip (Fig. 13). As you step forward with left foot, DRILL your left fist upward (Fig. 14), open it, and strike with it over your retreating right fist, which open palm down near your groin. Your left foot is now on a line slightly to the left (about a fist's width) of your right heel (Fig. 15). The length of your advancing step should accord with your height.

You are now in the *san-t'i* ("three essentials") posture, the basic Hsing-i posture, which generates both the FIVE FISTS and the TWELVE ANIMALS (Fig. 16). Your head should press up as if balancing a book, your elbows and shoulders should be held down, and your knees should be well bent, thus lowering your hips, forming a crease where your lower abdomen and thighs meet (the inguinal area). Your weight should be distributed so that the rear leg supports 60% of it. Your left arm should be extended, the elbow slightly bent and the fingertips at eyebrow level. Your left hand should be open and stretched to form the

12   13   14

INCORRECT

CORRECT

15. The Width of the Advancing Step in Hsing-i

16

"tiger mouth" as it strikes forward. Your open right hand should be held palm down, but the fingers pointed upward to protect the groin. Finally, your eyes look at your left index finger, gazing past it, focusing on a point ahead.

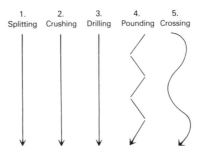

1.	2.	3.	4.	5.
Splitting	Crushing	Drilling	Pounding	Crossing

17. The Paths of the Five Fists

18   19   20

THE FIVE FISTS

1. SPLITTING FIST   (*P'i ch'uan*)

The SPLITTING FIST moves directly ahead (Fig. 17). Continuing from *san-t'i,* as you shift your weight rearward, retract both of your hands into fists downward as if pulling on a rope (Fig. 18). Take a small step forward with your left foot, toed out at 45° and DRILL forward with both fists as you shift your weight onto your left foot. Your left fist leads your right fist, DRILLING, and ends, palm up, at eyebrow level. Your right fist touches your left forearm between the wrist and the elbow (Fig. 19).

Next, suspend your right foot at your left ankle (Fig. 20). Then take a full step forward with your right foot, pushing off your left foot. (Kuo

21 22 23

24 25

Yun-shen said: "The rear foot holds strength as though you are going to leap off it across a ditch"; but step, don't jump.) Open your fists, palms down, SPLITTING your right hand over your retracting left, as all your weight shifts forward onto your right foot (Fig. 21). Next, follow-step a half-step forward with your left foot and shift 60% of your weight back to it (Fig. 22).

NOTE: All striking steps push off the rear foot and follow-
steps are always half-steps.

Repeat the posture on the other side by reversing the above directions. From the right *san-t'i* position, pull back and down with both hands (Fig. 23), DRILL both fists forward as you shift your weight forward to your toed-out right foot (Fig. 24), suspend your left foot at your right ankle (Fig. 25), and step forward with your left foot as you SPLIT for-

26   27   28

29   30

ward with your left palm, accompanied by your right palm in a two-handed chop (Fig. 26). Pull backward with your waist and two hands (Fig. 27), take a left toed-out step while screwing your palm-up fists forward, the left leading (Fig. 28). Then, suspending your right foot at your left ankle (Fig. 29), take it forward, accompanied by your right hand, while your left hand drops to protect your groin (Fig. 30).

To turn back, shift your weight to your left foot; then toe in your right foot and shift your weight to it while dropping your fists to your

31   32

33   34

hips (Fig. 31). Then take a half-step forward with your left foot, toed out, DRILL your fists forward, suspend your right foot at your left ankle and then take it a full step forward while SPLITTING with both palms forward (Figs. 32–34). After striking, shift 60% of your weight back to your left foot. Continue as before, and after two more repetitions, when your right foot and palm are ahead, you may turn around again. (Three postures in one direction are conventional, but five, seven, or more can be done if there is room.)

35   36   37

38   39

2. CRUSHING FIST (*Peng ch'uan*)

The CRUSHING FIST moves directly ahead (Fig. 17). From a left *san-t'i* (Fig. 35), begin to pull your left hand back to your left hip, clenching it into a palm-up fist. Simultaneously, begin to extend your right hand, clenching it into a vertical fist.

Take a short step directly forward with your left foot (Fig. 36), shift most of your weight to it, and CRUSH with your right fist directly ahead. Pay attention to retracting your left hand, thus augmenting the power of your right punch. Follow-step with your right foot and shift 60% of your weight back to it. Sit into the posture and maintain the inguinal fold (Fig. 37).

To alternate sides, take a half-step forward with your left foot, toed out 45° (Figs. 38, 39), suspend your right foot at your left ankle,

40   41   42

43   44   45

pause, and then take it forward (Figs. 40, 41). Simultaneously, retract your right fist, palm up, and CRUSH forward with your left fist (Fig. 42). After follow-stepping with your left foot, shift 60% of your weight back to it.

To turn back, shift most of your weight back to your left foot, toe-in your right foot, and bring your fists, palms down, to your hips (Fig. 43). Shift your weight to your right foot and take a half-step with your left foot, CRUSH ahead with your right fist while retracting your left fist, and follow-step with your right foot, shifting 60% of your weight back to it (Figs. 44, 45). Continue as before, doing another posture, so that your right foot and left fist are ahead before turning again. The number of repetitions is governed by space. In the CRUSHING fist, you must do any even number of repetitions before turning around.

46

47

48

3. DRILLING FIST (*Tsuan ch'uan*)

The DRILLING FIST moves directly ahead (Fig. 17). From a left *san-t'i* (Fig. 46), toe-out your left foot and shift all your weight to it while you raise your left palm high and circle inward. The palm should be held straight ahead of you, at eyebrow level, palm out, with fingers pointing to the right, as though depressing an opponent's strike. At the same time, retract your right hand, palm up, to your right hip and suspend your right foot at your left ankle (Fig. 47). There should be some tension of "pulling apart" between your left palm and your right fist.

Pushing off your left foot, step forward with your right foot and DRILL your right fist over your depressing left palm. Stop your right fist at eyebrow level and move your left palm, changed to a palm-down

49

50

fist, beneath your right elbow. Follow-step with your left foot and shift 60% of your weight back to it (Fig. 48).

To alternate sides, reverse the directions given above. Circle your right hand up to eyebrow level while taking a half-step forward with your toed-out right foot, suspending your left foot at your right ankle, and simultaneously retracting your palm-up left fist to your left hip (Fig. 49). After a brief pause, push off with your right foot, step forward with your left foot, and DRILL with your left fist, palm up, over your depressing right palm, which changes to a palm-down fist, beneath your left elbow (Fig. 50).

Next, take a half-step with your left foot forward while circling your left hand to eyebrow level, suspend your right foot at your left ankle,

51   52

and retract your palm-up right fist to your right hip (Fig. 51). Then step forward with your right foot, DRILLING your right fist to eyebrow level and moving your left palm, changed to a palm-down fist, beneath your right elbow. Follow-step with your left foot and shift 60% of your weight back to it (Fig. 52).

To turn back with your right fist ahead, simply toe-in your right foot and bring your palm-down right fist to your right hip. Step out with your toed-out left foot, circle your left palm up as before, and turn your right fist palm up at your right hip. At the same time, suspend your right foot at your left ankle briefly and take it forward while DRILLING your right fist, palm up, over your depressing left palm, which moves as a palm-down fist beneath your right elbow. Follow-step with your left foot and shift 60% of your weight back to it. Then, continue as before, doing two more repetitions before your right foot and palm are ahead and you can turn around again. Three postures are usually done here, but if there is room you can continue for five, seven, or any odd number of repetitions. The turning movements are identical with those described above.

53   54

55   56

4.   POUNDING FIST   (*P'ao ch'uan*)

The POUNDING FIST moves forward in a zig-zag fashion (Fig. 17). From a left *san-t'i* (Fig. 53), sink your weight into your right foot as you pull both hands down in palm-up fists to near your right hip, simultaneously suspending your left foot at your right ankle (Fig. 54).

Step with your left foot toward the left diagonal, pushing off your right foot while raising your left fist, palm in, and prepare to POUND with your vertical right fist (Fig. 55). As your weight shifts onto your left foot, turn your left forearm outward, deflecting an upper strike from an opponent, and POUND diagonally toward the left with your right vertical fist slightly lower than your shoulder (Fig. 56). Follow-step with the right foot as before, and shift 60% of your weight to it.

Alternate sides by shifting more weight to your right foot and taking

57

58

59

60

a half-step toward the diagonal with your left foot (Fig. 57). Chamber your fists, palm up, near your left side, and suspend your right foot at your left ankle (Fig. 58). Then take a full step toward the right diagonal with your right foot, raising your right fist, palm up (Fig. 59). Now, as your weight shifts onto your right foot and your right arm rotates upward in deflecting, POUND with your left vertical fist. Then follow-step with your left foot as before (Fig. 60).

To turn around, pivot on your heels, toeing-in your right foot and turning your left foot outward. Shift your weight fully to your left foot, chamber your fists to your left hip, and suspend your right foot at your left ankle. Now proceed as before, stepping with your right foot to the right diagonal while deflecting with your right arm and POUND with your left vertical fist. If space permits, you may do four, six, or any even number of repetitions before your next turn.

61   62

63   64

5. CROSSING FIST   (*Heng ch'uan*)

The CROSSING FIST moves forward in a wavy fashion (Fig. 17). From a left *san-t'i* (Fig. 61), step forward diagonally to the left with your left foot, pushing off your right foot (Fig. 62). As your left foot is put down with the toes pointing directly ahead, close your right hand into a fist and start swinging it across your body clockwise, passing your navel, palm down, while your left hand closes into a fist in front of you (Fig. 63).

As you shift more of your weight to your left foot, continue CROSSING your right arm out from under your left until your right fist is palm up. Simultaneously, withdraw your left fist, palm down, to a point near your navel. Follow-step with your right foot as before (Fig. 64).

65   66   67

68   69

To alternate sides, take a half-step diagonally to the left, placing your left foot down with the toes pointing straight ahead (Fig. 65) and suspend your right foot at your left ankle (Fig. 66). Next, move your right foot diagonally to the right, toes pointing straight ahead (Fig. 67), CROSSING your left fist counterclockwise, underneath and around the retracting right fist (Fig. 68) and out to eyebrow level. Your left fist ends palm up; your right fist, palm down (Fig. 69). Follow-step with your left foot as before.

To turn back, shift your weight to the left and toe-in your right foot. Now take a half-step ahead with your left foot and CROSS your right fist from under your retracting left fist, and follow-step with your right foot as before. Continue doing the CROSSING fist for as many repetitions as you like, turning back only when your right foot is forward. Thus, two, four, or any even number of repetitions may be done.

70

71

72

ENDING

By substituting the DRAGON STYLE for the turning maneuver for any of the FIVE FISTS, you can close and end that series. This is done by toeing-in your right foot and raising your right hand, opening it palm down at eyebrow level. Your left hand opens near your right elbow (Fig. 70). Toe-out your left foot, pivoting on your heel, and turn your torso leftward (Fig. 71). Bend your knees, transferring most of your weight to your left foot, and raise your right heel off the ground.

Simultaneously, press (SPLIT) forward with your right palm, fingers at eyebrow level, while your left palm follows your right elbow (Fig. 72). Next, toe-in your left foot slightly, put your right heel beside your

73   74

75   76

left and lower your hands, palms facing the *tan-t'ien* (Fig. 73). Inhale
and raise your arms out to the sides and upward as you twist your
body rightward (Fig. 74). Press your palms down the center of your
body and bend your knees together as you exhale (Fig. 75). Stand up
in the INFINITY POSTURE (Fig. 76).

30′   31′

LINKING THE FIVE FISTS

After practicing the FIVE FISTS independently, moving back and forth in a straight line, you may link them sequentially as you turn after each series. A standard integrated set might look like this:

1) SPLITTING FIST: 3 repetitions, turning into
2) CRUSHING FIST: 4 repetitions, turning into
3) DRILLING FIST: 3 repetitions, turning into
4) POUNDING FIST: 4 repetitions, turning into
5) CROSSING FIST: 4 repetitions, turning into
   DRAGON STYLE and INFINITY POSTURE, which
   close the entire set.

Only two repetitions are shown for the CRUSHING, POUNDING, and CROSSING FISTS, but the fact that the extra two repetitions are identical with the first two obviate the need to illustrate them. Note also that the DRAGON STYLE is done in the integrated form only after the CROSSING FIST, closing the entire set. Instead, you simply merge one FIST with the next after you turn.

For example, on the third step of the SPLITTING FIST, with your right hand and right foot forward (Fig. 30′), swing back leftward as

44'   45'   37'

47'   52'

31'   58'   59'

60′

56′

described above (Fig. 31′), take a short step with your left foot, and then do a CRUSHING FIST (Figs. 44′, 45′).

To change the CRUSHING FIST into the DRILLING FIST, when your right foot and left fist are forward (Fig. 37′), swing leftward, taking a short step ahead with the left foot and shifting your weight forward onto it; then suspend your right foot at your left ankle as you extend your left arm out ahead of your eyebrows (Fig. 47′).

To change the DRILLING FIST into the POUNDING FIST, when your right hand and right foot are forward (Fig. 52′), turn back leftward (Fig. 31′). Retract your left foot to your right ankle as you pull back with both hands (Fig. 58′) and then step ahead diagonally to the left as your hands deflect, striking in the POUNDING FIST (Figs. 59′, 60′).

Ending in the POUNDING FIST with your right foot and left fist forward (Fig. 56′), change into the CROSSING FIST by turning around

63'

64'

69'

70'

71'

72′   73′   74′

75′

76′

leftward as before, then move your left foot diagonally across to the left and swing your right fist clockwise under your left elbow, doing the CROSSING FIST (Figs. 63′, 64′).

Finally, to close the CROSSING FIST sequence and the entire set, when your left fist and right foot are forward (Fig. 69′), turn around leftward into the DRAGON STYLE as described above (Figs. 70′–75′) and end in the INFINITY POSTURE (Fig. 76′).

5

Practicing the Twelve Animal Styles

Because of his intelligence, man is superior to other animals. Physically, however, he is unable to match the fighting ability of most animals. To the fundamental FIVE FISTS, therefore, Hsing-i adds twelve styles derived from the fighting characteristics of twelve animals, some mythical. Quite aside from their combatant functions, these styles exercise all parts of the body vigorously, and, with the mind leading and the *ch'i* sunk to the *tan-t'ien,* make a rigorous training regimen.

The names, types, and arrangement of the TWELVE ANIMAL STYLES vary according to the different schools of Hsing-i. The order in which Ch'en P'an-ling taught them is as follows:

1) dragon;
2) tiger;
3) monkey;
4) horse;
5) water strider;
6) cock;
7) falcon;
8) swallow;
9) snake;
10) *t'ai* (a mythical bird);
11, 12) combined eagle and bear.

BEGINNING

As in the FIVE FISTS, face diagonally to the right, your heels touching and feet held 45° apart, the left foot pointing straight ahead (Fig. 77).

77   78

79   80

Raise your hands laterally, reaching above your head and gradually turn your palms down while turning your waist slightly rightward (Fig. 78). Press your arms down the front of your body, clenching your fists, palms down, at your navel, as you lower your body by bending your knees (Fig. 79). While shifting most of your weight onto your right foot, turn your waist leftward, DRILLING your right fist upward and forward, palm up, to eyebrow level (Fig. 80). Simultaneously, retract your left fist, palm down, to your left hip. Now, as you step forward with your left foot such that the heels of your feet are on parallel lines about a fist's width apart, DRILL your left fist upward, open it, and SPLIT with it over your retracting right fist, which opens, palm down, near your groin. You are now in *san-t'i*, the basic starting posture, with 60% of your weight on your rear foot (Fig. 81).

81

82

83

THE TWELVE STYLES

1. DRAGON STYLE *(Lung hsing)*

The DRAGON STYLE is a vigorous series of movements using vertical action from down to up and hardy leaps into a low, crouching form of the SPLITTING FIST.

From a left *san-t'i* (Fig. 81), shift your weight to your right leg and pull your hands back in fists as if pulling down on a rope. Bringing them across your waist toward the diagonal right rear, simultaneously retract your left foot and suspend it at your right ankle (Fig. 82). Continue by DRILLING your left fist upward to your head and your right fist upward to your left elbow. You are now facing sideways to the beginning posture (Fig. 83).

84 85 86

87 88 89

Next, turn your right fist over, opening it downward into a palm and SPLITTING it over your retracting left fist, which also opens and turns palm down. Simultaneously, lift your left foot and put it down toed-out in a scissor-step (Figs. 84, 85). You are now aligned to the right diagonal forward, your left hand at your right elbow. A triangle is formed by your right knee behind your left calf—but be careful not to bend your knees too much at first.

Now pull your hands back as you turn leftward (Fig. 86). DRILL your fists upward, and as they approach your middle begin to leap upward, carrying your arms high and forward, your right fist leading (Fig. 87). With your body in mid-air, open and extend your left hand,

90   91   92

93   94   95

turn it over, and SPLIT it out over your retracting right hand, which has also turned over, palm down. Simultaneously, alternate your right leg ahead of your left and land solidly in a scissor-step, toward the left diagonal (Figs. 88, 89).

Pulling your arms back and turning slightly rightward (Fig. 90), DRILL your hands upward, your left leading (Fig. 91), and leap up (Fig. 92), changing the lead leg in mid-air and landing solidly in a scissor-step, facing diagonally to the right, your right arm out (Fig. 93).

Pulling your arms back to your middle and turning slightly leftward (Fig. 94), shift your weight back to your right foot and move your left foot a half-step forward (Fig. 95). As your left foot drops, DRILL your

96   97   98

99   100   101

right fist upward, preparing to punch, and begin to swing your right leg forward (Fig. 96). Now, leap off your left foot, propelling your body directly forward, executing a right DRILLING punch and right stamping kick (Fig. 97).

Landing heel first on your toed-out left foot (Fig. 98), let your right leg drop forward and down into scissor-step (Fig. 99), turn your left hand over and SPLIT it over the retracting right hand as before, your body now oriented straight ahead (Fig. 100).

Shift your weight back to your left foot and take a half-step forward with your right foot. Clench your left hand into a fist and extend it slightly while clenching your right hand into a fist, palm up, at your hip. Simultaneously, suspend your left foot at your right ankle (Fig. 101).

102   103   104

105   106   107

Taking a full step forward with your left foot, do a right CRUSHING FIST while pulling your left fist back to your hip and follow-stepping with your right foot (Fig. 102). Turning back rightward, toe-in your left foot, and bring your fists, palms up, back to your hips (Fig. 103). Next, toe-out your right foot as you do a "snake" move with your right palm above it (Fig. 104), and, clenching your right palm into a fist, DRILL as your turn your knee out and wedge kick with your right foot (Fig. 105). Now put your right foot down toed-out, open both hands (Fig. 106), and, as you do a SPLITTING FIST with your left palm over your right straight ahead, lower your body by bending both knees into a scissor-step (Fig. 107).

Finally, bring the style to a close by taking a step to the right rear with the right foot and dropping your left arm on top of your right

108   109   110

111   112   113

(Fig. 108). Continue by lowering both arms (Fig. 109), and move your left foot to your right foot such that the heels touch. As you stand, raise your arms outward to shoulder level (Fig. 110) and bring them upward over your head as you turn your waist rightward (Fig. 111). Then, bending your knees together, press your hands down to your groin (Fig. 112). Lastly, stand up, facing diagonally to the right, taking your hands to your sides and raising your head slightly, your eyes up (Fig. 113). The ancients said that when you rest you should look up, which is good for health. This conventional close is done after each ANIMAL STYLE by bringing the right foot to the right rear and proceeding as outlined above. Once you have mastered the DRAGON STYLE starting from the left *san-t'i* position, do it from the right *san-t'i* position, reversing the directions above.

114   115   116

117   118   119

2. TIGER STYLE (*Hu hsing*)

The TIGER STYLE is done energetically, featuring an initial pull followed by a push.

From a left *san-t'i* (Fig. 114), move your right foot diagonally to the right (Fig. 115) as you pull your hands down in fists and turn your waist slightly rightward (Fig. 116). Suspend your left foot at your right ankle, your hands continuing in one motion from the pull and circling upward, palms down, to eyebrow level (Fig. 117). Turn leftward, hands dropping at eyebrow level, and step diagonally to the left with the left foot while extending your arms, the left slightly ahead of the right, with the "tiger's mouths" well open (Fig. 118). As you shift most of your weight back to your right foot, lower your hands slightly (Fig. 119).

120   121   122

123   124   125

Next, move your left foot a half-step forward diagonally to the left as your pull your hands down in fists to your left hip, and suspend your right foot at your left ankle (Fig. 120). Now raise your open hands, palm down, circularly upward to eyebrow level (Fig. 121) and turn your waist to face diagonally to the right (Fig. 122). Then take a step with the right foot diagonally to the right (Fig. 123), pressing your palms down, the right held slightly ahead of the left, stopping at chest level (Fig. 124).

To turn to go the other way, shift the weight onto your left foot and toe-in your right foot (Fig. 125). Next, shift the weight to your right foot and toe-out your left foot, turning your waist and swinging your arms leftward (Fig. 126). Take a step with your right foot diagonally to the right as you pull your fists to your right hip, and suspend your left

126 127 128

129 130 131

foot at your right ankle (Figs. 127, 128). Open your fists and raise your hands to eyebrow level (Fig. 129). Turn your waist to face diagonally to the left (Fig. 130), and step in that direction with your left foot, pressing your hands down to chest level, the left hand leading (Fig. 131). The press is done lightly, in contrast to the TIGER STYLE as taught in some other schools of Hsing-i, in which it is performed more powerfully. Practice the TIGER STYLE by alternating sides, zig-zagging from one diagonal to the other. The simple turn done with your right foot ahead, followed by one repetition of the form, is conventional for most of the ANIMAL STYLES. After one repetition in the new direction, ending with your left foot forward, step back with your right foot and do the closing as described at the end of the DRAGON STYLE (Figs. 108–13).

MONKEY

START - FINISH

1.

3.

N
W ● E
S

2.

4.

5.

132. Directions in MONKEY STYLE   133

3. MONKEY STYLE   (*Hou hsing*)

The MONKEY STYLE features retreating squats and advancing jumps to the four corners (Fig. 132).

Starting in a left *san-t'i* facing north (Fig. 133), circling out and down, retract your hands into fists, palms up, to your hips (Fig. 134), shift your weight onto your left foot, and step laterally to the right with your right foot as you do a right DRILLING FIST (Fig. 135). Without changing your fists, shift your weight onto the ball of your right foot and pivot on it until you face the northwest (NW) corner (Figs. 136, 137). This posture is fairly long, with your right foot holding at least 60% of your weight. As you move your right foot a long step backward, shoot your left palm out over your retracting right palm (Figs. 138, 139), and squat, toeing-in your left foot. Extend your left palm and hold your right palm under your left elbow (Fig. 140).

Now, toe-out your left foot, rise, and step toward the NW with your right foot as your right palm starts to spear over your retracting left palm (Figs. 141, 142). Continuing, hop off your right foot, following

134   135   136

137   138   139

140   141   142

143   144   145

146   147

through with your right palm, shooting forward and high (Figs. 143, 144). Your retracting left palm protects at your right elbow or under your chin, and your left knee is lifted high (Fig. 145). Next, lower your left foot and your arms to a left *san-t'i* facing NW (Figs. 146, 147).

Now, move your right foot laterally to the right as you use right DRILLING FIST (Figs. 148, 149), and pivot on the ball of your right foot until you face the southwest (SW) corner (Figs. 150, 151). Take a

148

149

150

151

152 153 154

full step backward with your right foot as before (Figs. 152, 153), squat, and toe-in your left foot slightly, extending your left palm as you retract your right palm under your left elbow (Fig. 154). Toeing out your left foot, step further to the SW with your right foot (Figs. 141, 142; although the photos of the sequence end here, we will refer to the previous photos illustrating the same position). Hopping on your right foot as before, spear your right palm over your retracting left palm (Figs. 143–45). Then, as you put your left foot down, extend your left arm and retract your right hand, moving into a left *san-t'i* position (Figs. 146, 147).

Using the photos for the previous two corners, go to the northeast (NE) corner, repeating the movement to *san-t'i*. Then repeat the movement to the southeast (SE) corner, ending in *san-t'i*.

To end, do the same sequence, going directly up the center. From *san-t'i* facing SE, step laterally to the right with your right foot and put it down opposite your left foot, doing a right DRILLING FIST. Bring your weight to your right foot and pivot as before (Figs. 136, 137) so that you face the front center in a right forward stance, your hands staying fixed as before. Now step back and squat on your right leg. Next, hop forward on your right foot while spearing with your right hand. Then lower your left foot and your hands into a left *san-t'i* position. Finally, step back with your right foot and do the conventional close.

For balance, after mastering the MONKEY STYLE from this side, begin with the right *san-t'i* position and do it from the other side doing the four corners in the sequence NE, SE, NW, and SW.

155

156

157

4. HORSE STYLE (*Ma hsing*)

The HORSE STYLE is a speedy and powerful posture in which the fists, palms down, strike together as you move forward in a zig-zag path.

From a left *san-t'i* (Fig. 155), as you step forward diagonally to the right with your right foot, change both hands into palm-up fists and bring them together, forearms close, swinging them straight down in front of your *tan-t'ien*. Simultaneously, suspend your left foot at your right ankle (Fig. 156).

Continue swinging your arms out laterally, fists on a line with your lower ribs (Fig. 157). Pause, then turn your arms over from the elbows, until your fists, palms down, line up with your shoulders. Hang your elbows and hold your right fist near your left elbow. Turning your waist leftward, step ahead diagonally to the left with your left

158   159   160

161   162

foot and punch forward with both "flat" fists, your left fist slightly ahead (Fig. 158). Finally, bring your right foot forward in a follow-step and shift 60% of your weight back onto it (Fig. 159). Use your waist: your navel should point directly ahead on the short steps and 45° on the long steps.

Continuing, step forward diagonally to the left with your left foot (Fig. 160) and suspend your right foot at your left ankle while swinging your arms down and out (Figs. 161, 162). Now, turn the waist, step diagonally to the right with your right foot, and circle your "flat" fists up and forward, your right held slightly ahead (Fig. 163). Follow-step with your left foot, shifting 60% of your weight back to it (Fig. 164).

163

164

Continue the alternate zig-zag step for four repetitions until your right leg is ahead. Turn back leftward and shift your weight to your left foot as you toe-in your right foot. Continue by shifting your weight back and toe-out your left foot. Next, step ahead diagonally to the right with your right foot and change both hands to palm-up fists and bring them together, forearms close, swinging them straight down in front of your *tan-t'ien*. Simultaneously, suspend your left foot at your right ankle (refer back to Fig. 156). Turn your arms over as before, turn your waist, and step ahead diagonally to the left with your left foot as you punch with both ''flat'' fists, your left slightly ahead (refer back to Figs. 157–159). Finally, step back a short step with your right foot and do the conventional close.

165 166

167 168

5. WATER STRIDER STYLE (*T'ou hsing*)

The WATER STRIDER STYLE resembles the "Cloud Hands" (*Yun shou*) posture of T'ai-chi and emphasizes the flexibility of the waist.   From a left *san-t'i* (Fig. 165), retract your left foot and suspend it at your right ankle while circling your left hand down counterclockwise as you turn your waist rightward (Fig. 166), stopping your left fist in front of your eyes (Fig. 167). Hold your right fist, palm down, at your navel. You are now facing sideways from the *san-t'i* position. Step ahead diagonally to the left with your left foot and roll your waist leftward, carrying your left arm, held at a right angle, across your body (Fig. 168).

Continue turning your waist and left fist, palm in, leftward, shifting your weight to your left foot. As the hand passes the front, turn it out-

169

170

171

172

173

ward in a half-clenched fist while keeping your right fist, palm down, at your *tan-t'ien*, and suspend your right foot at your left ankle (Fig. 169).

Alternate sides by turning your waist rightward as you take your right fist inside your extended left arm in a clockwise circle (Fig. 170), at the same time stepping ahead diagonally to the right with your right foot (Fig. 171). Continue rolling your waist rightward until your right half-clenched fist is in front of your eyes, your left fist is at your *tan-t'ien*, and your body is turned past the center to the right (Fig. 172).

Continue the alternating zig-zag step for four repetitions until your right leg is ahead, when you can turn around. Toe-in your right foot as you circle your right fist to your *tan-t'ien*, next to your left fist (Fig. 173). Next, withdraw your left foot and suspend it at your right ankle as you screw your left fist up ahead of your body at eyebrow level (Fig. 174). Turning leftward, move your left foot diagonally to the left (Fig.

174

175

176

175), and, as you shift your weight to your left foot, turn your left forearm outward in deflection as your right fist, palm down, stays at your *tan-t'ien*, and suspend your right foot at your left ankle (Fig. 176). Finally, step back with your right foot and do the conventional close.

177 178 179

180 181

6. COCK STYLE (*Chi hsing*)

The COCK STYLE stresses strong legs and adroit arms.

From a left *san-t'i* (Fig. 177), shift more of your weight back to your right foot and let your left heel come off the ground as you relax your arms, raising your right hand to near your left elbow, and drooping the fingers of both hands (Fig. 178). Take a half-step directly forward with your left foot (Fig. 179), and, as you shift your weight onto it, move your right palm beneath your left forearm up and forward, suspending your right foot at your left ankle (Figs. 180, 181). Pause, drooping your hands slightly.

182

183

184

Then step forward with your right foot and move your left palm beneath your right forearm up and forward (Fig. 182), while suspending your left foot at your right ankle (Fig. 183). Pause.

Then raise your arms slightly (Fig. 184) and step forward with your left foot (Fig. 185), pressing down with both palms (Fig. 186). Follow-step with your right foot and do a left *san-t'i*.

Do four repetitions of the COCK STYLE, moving in a straight line. After the first repetition, it is not necessary to shift your weight back and droop your arms as shown in Figure 178. Simply shift your weight forward onto your left foot and repeat the movement as shown above (Fig. 186).

Turn around by pivoting on your heels 180° rightward so that you face the opposite direction in the right *san-t'i* position. Then do the

185

186

COCK STYLE four times in the other direction by reversing the instructions above. As a standard form, however, starting from the left *san-t'i* position, do a series of four repetitions and then, with your left foot forward, turn around 180° into the right *san-t'i* position and do one repetition. Finally, move your leading right foot backward and do the conventional close. Alternatively, you may practice as many repetitions as you have room to do in each direction.

187 188

189 190

7. FALCON STYLE (*Yao hsing*)

The FALCON STYLE is sharp and emphasizes the fist used with both a contracted and an opened body.

From the left *san-t'i* position (Fig. 187), withdraw and sink, emptying your left foot. Change your hands into fists, moving your right fist, palm up, to your right hip and lowering your left standing fist on a line with your left leg (Fig. 188).

Shift your weight to your left foot and move your right foot forward, pausing above your left ankle (Fig. 189). Now, as you stamp your right foot down, punch with a standing right fist over your left fist and suspend your left foot at your right ankle (Fig. 190).

As you step forward with your left foot, arc both arms outward and

191

192

193

down, the right inside the left (Figs. 191, 192). Shift your weight to your left foot as you drop your fists, your right slightly higher than your left. Your left fist should align with your left ear; your right fist, with your eyebrows. Then look at your right hand and shift your weight so that you are 60% rear-weighted (Fig. 193).

After repeating the FALCON STYLE several times on one side, turn around by toeing in your left leading foot and toeing out your rear foot and going in the other direction, using your left fist and stamping with your left foot. As a standard form, however, starting from the left *san-t'i* position, do a series with your right fist and foot, turn around and do one with your left fist and foot, and finish by moving the leading right foot backward past the left and doing the conventional close.

194   195

196   197   198

8. SWALLOW STYLE (*Yen hsing*)

The SWALLOW STYLE is an invigorating blend of soaring and squatting.

From a left *san-t'i* (Fig. 194), step forward with your right foot, toed-out, depressing forward and down with your right hand as you press with your left hand under your right elbow (Fig. 195). Shift all of your weight onto your right foot and lift your left leg, holding the foot before the right knee with toes pointing down, as you begin a large clockwise circle with your right drooping hand (Fig. 196). Turn your waist rightward, your right hand at eyebrow level (Fig. 197), and put your left foot down ahead, shifting 40% of your weight onto it. You should now be turned toward the right and looking at your right index finger (Fig. 198).

199

200

201

202

As you shift most of your weight to your left foot, your right hand continues circling around and down past the right side of your body (Fig. 199), and, as your weight goes fully onto your left leg, raise your right hand as before, but this time with your right foot held suspended before your left knee (Fig. 200).

Turn your waist rightward and move your right hand, palm out, in another circle, your left hand accompanying it by pivoting from the left elbow (Fig. 201). When your hands are at the highest point, jump off your left foot and land on your right foot as you extend your right hand backward from its circle, changing it into a "pecking hand" (similar to that used in the "Single Whip" [*tan-pien*] posture of T'ai-chi). Hold your left hand near your right elbow and left knee high, the left foot held before the right knee with toes pointing down (Fig. 202).

203

204

205

206

207

208

209

210

Now extend your left foot to the front, dropping most of your weight onto your right leg, sinking into a low squat. Stretch your left hand, palm down, down along your left leg to your ankle. Simultaneously, turn your right "pecking hand" over toward the rear, so that the fingers point up (Fig. 203).

Rise and shift your weight to your left leg, bringing your right hand, palm up, to your right hip while extending your left hand slightly, palm down (Fig. 204). Now step forward with your right foot and begin to raise your right hand, palm up (Fig. 205). Move your right hand, stabbing forward and upward to shoulder level as your weight shifts fully to your right leg, your left foot suspended at your right ankle. Simultaneously, slap your right forearm with your left palm (Fig. 206).

Next, change your open hands into fists (Fig. 207), step forward with your left foot, and punch directly ahead with a left CRUSHING FIST. At the same time, retract your right fist, palm up, to your right hip and follow-step with your right foot (Fig. 208).

Toe-out your left foot, raise your left hand, palm down (Fig. 209), and take a full step forward with your right foot while doing a right DRILLING FIST over your depressing left hand. Change your left open hand into a palm-down fist at your right elbow as you follow-step with your left foot. Your weight is now 60% backloaded (Fig. 210).

After performing one SWALLOW STYLE movement, with your right foot ahead in the DRILLING FIST, turn leftward to face the other direction by toeing-in your right foot and toeing-out your left foot, keeping your hands in the DRILLING FIST position. Then drop your hands and step back with your right foot in the conventional close.

For free practice, if there is room enough, you may simply step forward with your left foot past the DRILLING FIST into the left *san-t'i* position and do another SWALLOW STYLE form, repeating the directions above. If there is insufficient room, turn around after each repetition and do it going in the opposite direction. Because of its complexity, do the SWALLOW STYLE only from a left *san-t'i* until you master it, and then try it from a right *san-t'i*, reversing the directions given above.

211

212

213

9. SNAKE STYLE   (*She hsing*)

The SNAKE STYLE stresses elasticity and palms shooting up from a crouching posture.

From the left *san-t'i* position (Fig. 211), retract your left foot and suspend it at your right ankle. Pivoting at the left elbow, move the forearm in a small arc and pierce down the center of your body. Turn your left palm so that it faces your left knee and raise your right palm so that it protects your left shoulder (Fig. 212).

Turn your left hand over so that the palm faces out (Fig. 213), and step directly forward with your left foot (Fig. 214). As your right foot follow-steps, your forward momentum carries your left hand upward, striking with the wrist-top, while your right hand retracts to your right

214

215

216

hip (Fig. 215). Sink slightly, shifting your weight back onto your right leg, and snap your left hand upward from the wrist. You now hold your right hand, palm down, at your right hip (Fig. 216).

Alternate sides by taking a half-step with your left foot, toed out, and slicing your right hand down the center of your body, reversing the directions above. Do four repetitions. With your right foot and hand forward, toe-in your right foot and turn back leftward to the other direction with your left foot in the left *san-t'i* position. Drop back as shown in Figure 212, and do one repetition of the SNAKE STYLE form, ending with your left foot forward, as shown in Figure 216. Lastly, step back with your right foot and do the conventional close.

217   218

219   220

10.   T'AI STYLE   (*T'ai hsing*)

The T'AI (a mythical bird) STYLE briskly zig-zags forward while generating power by an initial circling of the arms upward, in contrast to the HORSE STYLE'S initial circling downward.

From a left *san-t'i* (Fig. 217), take a step forward diagonally to the right with your right foot (Fig. 218) and raise your right arm under your left, both forearms going overhead as your left foot follows to suspend at your right ankle (Fig. 219). Pull your arms apart, completing the circle, stopping your fists, palms up, at your hips (Fig. 220). Turn your waist leftward and step forward diagonally to the left with your left foot (Fig. 221), and punch down with your right fist, palm down, over your extended palm-down left fist. Follow-step and shift your weight back to your rear foot (Fig. 222).

221

222

To alternate sides, take a half-step with your left foot further along the left diagonal, suspending your right foot at your left ankle, raise your arms, left under right, and circle out and down, stopping at your hips, palms up. Then turn your waist rightward and step with your right foot to the diagonal as you punch with your left fist, palm down, over your right fist.

After four repetitions on this zig-zag path, you end with your right foot forward and your body facing diagonally to the right. To turn back leftward to the other direction, toe-in your right foot, toe-out your left foot, and step to the right front with your right foot, circling your arms, and suspend your left foot at your right ankle. Pause and then take a step directly forward with your left foot and punch with right "flat" fist over your left arm, follow-step with your right foot, and shift 60% of your weight back onto it. Finally, step further back with your right foot and do the conventional close.

223

224

225

11. & 12.   COMBINED EAGLE-AND-BEAR STYLE
(*Ying-Hsiung hsing*)

The COMBINED EAGLE-AND-BEAR STYLE integrates the properties of yin and yang, the straight and the oblique, and the up and the down; it also features the SPLITTING FIST done diagonally.

From a left *san-t'i* (Fig. 223), copy the first part of the DRAGON STYLE: Shift your weight to your right leg and pull your hands back in fists as if pulling on a rope. Bringing them across your waist toward the right hip. Simultaneously, retract your left foot and suspend it at your right ankle (Fig. 224). DRILL your left fist upward to your head, and your right fist upward at your left elbow. You are now in a position sideways to the beginning posture (Fig. 225).

Next, turn your right fist over, opening it palm downward, and

226

227

228

SPLIT it over your retracting left hand, which opens and turns palm-down. Simultaneously, lift your left foot and put it down, toed-out, in a scissor-step (Fig. 226). You are now aligned to the right diagonal forward, your left hand at your right elbow. Keep the triangle formed by your right knee behind your left calf—but be careful not to bend your knees too much at first.

Take a half-step with your left foot diagonally across to the right and pull your hands back into palm-up fists at your left hip (Fig. 227). As you shift your weight onto your left foot, DRILL your right fist upward and high diagonally to the left, your left fist following your right elbow. Simultaneously, suspend your right foot at your left ankle (Fig. 228).

Now step further diagonally to the right with your right foot as you

229   230   231

232   233

234   235   236

237

238

open your left hand and press it forward, SPLITTING over your right palm (Fig. 229). As your right foot goes down, stop your left palm at eye level and your right palm at your *tan-t'ien*. Follow-step with your left foot (Fig. 230).

Alternate sides by stepping with your right foot diagonally across to the left as you pull your hands to your right hip (Fig. 231). Then, suspending your left foot at your right ankle, DRILL your left fist diagonally to the right (Fig. 232). Now step further diagonally to the left with your left foot, SPLITTING your right palm over your left palm (Figs. 233, 234).

Next, do a third repetition, pulling your hands leftward as you step rightward with your left foot (Fig. 235), suspending your right foot and DRILLING your right fist (Fig. 236). Finish off by stepping out with your right foot while SPLITTING your left palm over your right palm and follow-stepping with your left foot (Figs. 237, 238).

Turn and do one repetition in the other direction to complete the

239 240

241 242

form. To turn around, toe-in your right foot and toe-out your left foot
(Fig. 239), and step diagonally toward the right with your left foot as
you retract your fists to your left hip (Fig. 240). Now DRILL with your
right fist diagonally to the the left and suspend your right foot as before
(Fig. 241). Then, open your left fist and SPLIT it over your retracting
right hand as you put your right foot down. As before, your left palm
stops at eyebrow level and your right palm at the *tan-t'ien* (Fig. 242).
Finally, step backward with your right foot and do a conventional
close.

PART THREE

Introduction to Pa-kua Boxing

6
What Is Pa-kua?

She moved in circles,
and those circles moved. . . .

—T. Roethke
"I Knew a Woman"

PHILOSOPHY AND PRACTICE

Pa-kua, pronounced "ba-gwa," is one of the three martial arts that comprise the internal system (*nei-chia*) of Chinese boxing. The theory of Pa-kua, based on the *Book of Changes (I Ching),* is difficult, but actualized as *Pa-kua chang* (Pa-kua Palm), a boxing-meditational exercise, it is even more difficult. Done to cultivate the *tao* (the way), the circling movements of Pa-kua both manifest Heaven and Earth and order and organize *yin* and *yang.* They follow the seasons and benefit man. When practicing Pa-kua, you walk the circle as though macrocosmically walking in the universe, affecting and being affected microcosmically by the changes inside your body.

The name as well as the rationale of Pa-kua derive from the system of philosophy that gave rise to the *Book of Changes*—an ancient metaphysical treatise over three thousand years old but timeless in its wisdom. Originally a manual of oracles, the *Book of Changes* evolved into a compilation of ethical enumerations, eventually becoming such a compendium of knowledge that it was chosen as one of the Five

Classics of Confucianism. It became a common source for both Confucian and Taoist philosophy. The central theme of the book, as well as of the system of boxing, is that everything is in flux. While the book's basic idea is the continuous process of change underlying all existence, Pa-kua has absorbed these ideas and transmuted them into a system of exercise and self-defense.

Originally, the *Book of Changes* contained a collection of linear signs meant to be used as oracles. In the most rudimentary sense, these oracles confined themselves to the answers "yes" and "no." Thus, "yes" was symbolized by a single unbroken *yang* line (———), and "no" by a single broken *yin* line (— —). Time brought a need for differentiation and amplification, which required additional lines. Thus, the eight trigrams (or units of three lines ☰) evolved, and at a later date these were further expanded to create the sixty-four hexagrams (or units of six lines ䷀). The Chinese word for such a combination of lines is *kua* (diagram). This, then, is the origin of the word Pa-kua— the eight trigrams.

The eight trigrams that form the basis of the *Book of Changes* are as follows:

Name	Attribute	Image	Part of Body
Ch'ien, Creative	Strong	Heaven	Head, heart
K'un, Receptive	Yielding	Earth	Spleen, stomach
Chen, Arousing	Movement	Thunder	Liver, throat
K'an, Abysmal	Dangerous	Water	Kidneys, ears
Ken, Stillness	Resting	Mountain	Back, hands/feet
Sun, Gentle	Penetrating	Wind	Intestines
Li, Clinging	Brilliance	Fire	Heart, spirit
Tui, Joyous	Joyful	Lake	Lungs, chest

In turn, these trigrams are often arranged in a circle around a T'ai-chi (Great Ultimate) symbol, the familiar diagram divided into *yin* and *yang* (Fig. 1). As the two *yin* and *yang* lines combine into groups of three, they gather at the eight directions to form the eight trigrams.

1. The Pa-kua Diagram

The sixty-four hexagrams evolved from the combinations of the eight trigrams being paired with one another. The theory behind this is explained in the *Book of Changes,* where the trigrams are also identified with the human body.

The diagram of the eight trigrams shown in Figure 1 is based upon the philosophy of the *Book of Changes.* The symbology is broad enough to embrace all things in Heaven and Earth, and narrow enough to represent the workings of the human body. It forms a path that can be followed both in cultivating the *tao* and in studying Pa-kua boxing. It also forms the essence of Pa-kua: "If you do not understand the philosophical theory expounded by the diagram, but only perform the movements of Pa-kua," Wang Shu-chin writes, "you will merely be doing calisthenics."

The basic eight trigrams from the *Book of Changes* are correlated with the fundamental eight Pa-kua forms as follows:

1. ☰ **Ch'ien,** the Creative principle, is associated with strength and the image of Heaven. We learn from Nature: Heaven is great because it moves without stopping. The SINGLE CHANGE OF PALM, similarly, is continuous and smooth and promotes blood circulation. Practiced incorrectly, it can hurt the heart.

2. ☲ **Li,** the Clinging principle, is brilliant and is associated with fire, which adheres to whatever it burns. To do the DOUBLE CHANGE OF PALM correctly, you should be internally soft and externally hard, like a snake wriggling into its hole. If done correctly, this form will help you to feel united with the universe.

3. ☳ **Chen,** the Arousing principle, incites movement and vibration and is associated with thunder. When practicing HAWK SOARS UP TO HEAVEN, keep your upper body soft and lower body hard, externally quiet yet internally moving. Though still, you have the potential to move, and your enemy will be misled by your seeming lack of movement. Physically, the *ch'i* of your liver will be harmonized rather than agitated if you perform this form correctly.

4. ☷ **K'un,** the Receptive principle, is associated with yielding and with the Earth. YELLOW DRAGON ROLLS OVER stresses the unity of the upper and lower body, of the internal and the external. Practiced correctly, this form will make your body feel as light and agile as that of a fine horse.

5. ☵ **K'an,** the Abysmal principle, is associated with danger and with water. It indicates that in the midst of trouble you must persevere with self-confidence, which will lead to success. WHITE SNAKE STICKS OUT TONGUE stresses an appearance of softness but with a strong inner core: a strong mind and a soft hand movement. Practiced correctly, the form will help you to feel calm and centered, and will keep you from becoming dizzy.

6. ☶ **Ken,** the Stillness principle, represents the state of rest and is associated with mountains. When a bowl rests upside down, you cannot see what is in it. GIANT ROC SPREADS WINGS shows a tendency to be motionless. Practiced correctly, it will reduce the fire in your heart and enable your *ch'i* to reach the four extremities.

7. ☱ **Tui,** the Joyous principle, is associated with lowness and with lakes. In doing WHITE MONKEY PRESENTS A PEACH, keep your upper body soft and your middle and lower parts hard. Lower your body like a tiger squatting, prepared to pounce. Practiced correctly, this form will help your lungs to feel clear and will keep you from panting.

8. ☴ **Sun,** the Gentle principle, is associated with penetrating and with the wind, which can penetrate any opening. WHIRL-WIND PALMS is characterized by a strong top and a soft bottom, and the body turns like a wheel. Done correctly, this form will help your *ch'i* penetrate every part of your body and make your movements as fast as the wind.

HISTORY AND MASTERS

The origin of Pa-kua is unknown. The first specific reference to it is 1796, when it was recorded that a boxer in Shantung named Wang Hsiang taught the art to a certain Feng Ke-shan. In 1810 Feng met a

Niu Liang-ch'en, who also taught him certain aspects of the art. The traditional teaching, however, is that Tung Hai-ch'uan (1798–1879) of Hopei Province is its modern progenitor.

Tung Hai-ch'uan was a poor boy from Hopei province who, after some scrapes in Peking, journeyed to Mount Omei in Szechwan Province, where he met two Taoists, Ku Chi-tzu and Shang Tao-yuan (the surnames are standard but the given names have strong Taoist connotations, and hence are probably ''religious'' names), who taught him Pa-kua for eleven years. For seven years he reportedly walked around a tree until it seemed to lean toward him, at which time he became enlightened and reported his experience to the Taoists. They then had him do a figure-8 walk circling two trees, which he did for two years until it seemed that the trees began to ''pursue'' him. The Taoists praised him and asked if he were homesick. When he acknowledged that he was, they congratulated him on not losing his natural feelings and then taught him hand changes and weapons techniques for two years, after which he returned home to Hopei and then went to Peking, where he taught a number of students.

After becoming famous in Peking, Tung was challenged by Kuo Yun-shen (''Divine Crushing Hand'') of the Hsing-i tradition. Throughout two whole days of fighting, Kuo, feared for having killed a man with his famous ''crushing'' hand, could not gain any advantage. On the third day, Tung took the offensive and so completely defeated Kuo that the two became lifelong friends. They were so impressed with each other's level of accomplishment that they signed a brotherhood pact requiring all their students to train in the other's discipline as well. For this reason—a most unusual outcome for any fight—both Pa-kua and Hsing-i are to this day coupled and complementary.

About the time of the T'ai Ping Rebellion (1850–64), Tung is thought to have been involved in a revolt against the foreign Manchu government, after which he escaped by fleeing to Peking and became an official in the Imperial court. He did not get along with the other officials, however, and was soon thereafter transferred to the household of Prince Su, a relative of Ching-dynasty emperor T'ung Chih (r. 1862–75), to work as a servant, since no one knew of his prowess as a Pa-kua master. Prince Su employed Sha Hui-tsu, a Moslem boxer, as the Chief of the Royal Guards who protected his residence. Sha held every member of the household staff to strict and immediate obedience, and his wife, an expert with a pistol, effectively reinforced her husband's orders. Once, at a crowded banquet, Tung served tea to the guests by lightly scaling the wall and crossing the roof to the kitchen and back. Prince Su recognized from this that Tung must have great ability in some martial art, and subsequently ordered Tung to show his art. Unable to refuse, he demonstrated Pa-kua. His sudden turns and flowing style enthralled the audience. Seeing that, Sha challenged Tung to a fight but was soundly defeated. Thereafter, Tung watched for Sha to try to get revenge. Late one night Sha crept into Tung's bedroom, knife in hand, while his wife aimed her pistol at Tung through the window. Before they were even aware that he was moving, Tung had taken the pistol away from the wife and stood there pointing it at Sha, who thereupon fell to his knees and pounded his head on the floor seeking forgiveness. Tung not only forgave him; he accepted him as a student.

As he aged, he felt the need to pass Pa-kua on and so he retired and began to teach Pa-kua to a few select students. Although Tung gradually withered, the stories about him did not. One tells of how he once found himself surrounded by a group of thugs trying to kill him— but he not only emerged unscathed; he actually defeated the whole band of attackers. Another relates that once Tung was sitting in a chair leaning against a wall when the wall collapsed. His disciples, fearing that he has been buried alive, rushed in looking for him, and found him sitting in the same chair, leaning against another wall! A similar anecdote tells of how he was napping one autumn day and, as the air was quite chilly, his disciples picked up a sheet and quietly tried to cover him. When they put the sheet down, however, there was no one there! "What's the matter with you?" asked Tung's voice from where he was sitting near the window. "Why did you try to startle me?"

But perhaps the grandest story, which is told by Wan Lai-sheng, concerns Tung's death. Certain that he was dead, some of his students attempted to raise the casket prior to the funeral. But it would not budge; it remained as though solidly riveted to the ground. As his students tried again and again to lift it—in vain—a voice came from within, saying: "As I've often said, none of you has even one-tenth my skill!" He then passed away, and the casket was moved easily. Tung died at 81.

Pa-kua emerged from the hidden Taoist ranks first with Tung and only reached the general public after 1900. Among a reported total of only 72, Tung's most famous students were Yin Fu, Ch'eng T'ing-hua, Ma Wei-chi, Liu Feng-ch'un, and Shih Liu.

Yin Fu (nicknamed "Thin Yin") was a native of I-hsien in Hopei Province. Though he had superior skill, he taught few students. He guarded a nobleman's residence for a living and died in 1909 at 69.

Ch'eng T'ing-hua, also a native of Hopei, was nicknamed "Invincible Cobra Ch'eng." Besides teaching Pa-kua, he ran a shop in Peking that sold spectacles, whence he derived his nickname "Cobra." (Europeans, as well, refer to the cobra as the "eyeglass snake"; in German, it is called *brillenschlange*.) One story relates that during the Western occupation of Peking at the time of the Boxer Rebellion (1900), when the foreigners were looting, raping, and killing, Ch'eng rushed out of his house with a knife concealed under each armpit and killed at least a dozen German soldiers before being shot to death. (This story is probably apocryphal, however, since other, more reliable sources assert that he died a natural death past the age of 70.) Another tale tells of how he killed one of his senior students, a man named Ma, who had attacked him while he was in bed.

Ch'eng's top students included Li Ts'un-i, Sun Lu-t'ang, Chang Yu-kuei, Han Ch'i-ying, Feng Chun-i, K'an Ling-feng, Chou Hsiang, Li Han-chang, Li Wen-piao, and Ch'in Ch'eng. Li Ts'un-i, also gifted in Hsing-i, is sometimes recorded as being a direct student of Tung Hai-ch'uan, but his name does not appear on the list engraved on Tung's gravestone. Li, nonetheless, was quite famous and taught thousands in Peking.

Sun Lu-t'ang (1859–1933) learned all three of the internal martial arts, studying Pa-kua under Ch'eng T'ing-hua. Though his interests were diverse, and though he is remembered chiefly for his books—which opened up these arts to the public—he was also a great fighter. Once in Pao-ting, a wrestling stronghold, two opponents simultaneously attacked him, one kicking and one striking. Sun deflected both attacks, and the men were thrown yards away, although bystanders never saw Sun exert any force. At 70, at a boxing meeting, he challenged all present to try to hold on to his finger. Whenever a strong boxer grabbed him with a tight grip, he circularized his *ch'i,* easily extracting the digit from anyone's grasp. Sun's daughter, still alive and teaching T'ai-chi in Peking, recently said that although her father was famous for his fighting, she still remembers how nervous he was a week before a match with a Japanese challenger. He was restless and on edge, awaiting the day. It came, he quickly disposed of the Japanese, and then became his usual calm self again.

Ma Wei-chi, another of Tung's best students, taught Sung Yung-hsiang, Sung Ch'ang-jung, Liu Feng-ch'un, Liang Chen-pu, Chang Chao-tung, and Wang Li-te. Some sources believe that Ma was actually taught by Ch'eng T'ing-hua rather than by Tung himself.

Chang Chao-tung, another native of Hopeh Province, was an expert in both Hsing-i and Pa-kua. Each year Chang returned to his home in Hochien Hsien from Tientsin to visit his parents. The year he turned 60, he returned to find a 40-year-old man named Ma installed as the village's leading boxer. Ma approached Chang and politely told him that he could withstand his punch. (This was the usual way of deciding who was the stronger boxer—each would get a free swing at the other's body. The loser, however, had the choice of challenging for an actual contest if unsatisfied with the one-punch method.) Chang obliged smilingly but ordered four students to hold up a blanket behind Ma. Then he told Ma: "Hold up your hands to protect your body; I will hit only your arm." So saying, Chang hit Ma's arm with his fingers and the back of his hand. Ma immediately fell back sharply into the blanket, pulling all four students atop him. Ma knelt down at once and became a disciple of Chang's.

Wang Shu-chin, the master whose circling method is presented here, started receiving instruction at 18 under the famed Chang Chao-tung in 1923 (Fig. 2). In 1934 he spent a year studying stake standing (*chang chuang*) under Wang Hsiang-chai. Both were "highly skilled, morally upright, and strict taskmasters," he writes in his *Pa-kua Lien-huan Chang* (Pa-kua Linked Palm; Taipei, 1978; privately published. The historical data on Tung Hai-ch'uan are gleaned from this book, and differ somewhat from other accounts. Wang studied in a direct line of succession from Tung, through Ma Wei-chi and Chang Chao-tung; hence, the information he gives is probably more accurate).

Five years later, in 1939, he studied under the 90-year-old veteran Hsiao Hai-po, a master who had studied near Mount Omei in Szechwan, a man who "as a person was genial and cultivated, as a teacher untiring, truly a model for our generation."

Through these years, Wang "avoided entanglements, followed vegetarianism and Taoism, meditated, and practiced boxing." He

2. Wang Shu-chin, Walking the Pa-kua Circle

taught all three internal arts but restricted his Hsing-i and Pa-kua instruction to dedicated students in Taiwan. In the 1960s and 1970s, he went to Japan eight times to teach Tai-chi, and by the time he died in 1981 he had taught nearly 2,000 students, some 1,200 of them in Japan, where he had even opened a branch of his school that still teaches his forms. He was not only a teacher, but a friend. It was his wish that the right method be transmitted in the right way. Therefore, we have taken care to present his method of Pa-kua in a way that we think would have pleased him.

7
Essential Pa-kua

The gulf between what you have already learned and classical Pa-kua is great. The fundmental eight forms of Pa-kua given in this book, with their emphasis on the circular, employ a chiefly *horizontal* strength, in contrast to the mainly linear Hsing-i forms, which develop a more *vertical* strength. If someone attacks you on a straight line with body and legs advancing, that is *vertical* strength. But if you intercept the arm laterally and counterattack on a curving line with your body rotating, that is *horizontal* strength. To help explain the intricacies of classical Pa-kua, we would like to pass on some of the advice given to Mr. Smith by Kuo Feng-ch'ih, under whom he trained for more than two years. The concepts expressed below are intrinsic to all three internal arts and are in accord with the principles of the art as taught by Wang. Thus, if you understand these ideas, you will comprehend the rationale of T'ai-chi and Hsing-i, as well as Pa-kua.

SUBSTANCE AND FUNCTION

To eradicate any erroneous ideas you may have, let us compare both the *internal* and the *external* types of martial arts. If we examine the substance and function of the two types of boxing, we will see that there is a great difference between them.

All *internal* styles are based on the combined training of body and spirit, as exemplified in Taoist doctrines, the main goal of which is to achieve a state of being without any desire or belligerent attitude, neither self-abasing nor arrogant, always advancing and indomitable. In the *internal* styles, ''spiritual'' cultivation and the nurturing of *ch'i* are primary, but boxing theory, technique, and practice must also be accorded their due. When the need arises, the ''spiritual'' cultivation is transmuted into physical activity in exactly the right amount needed to protect you from harm.

All the *external* styles, however, place more stress on the physical training aspect, emphasizing muscle size and strength, as well as the achievement of impractical feats of physical prowess. They tend to flamboyant displays and demonstrations of sheer strength.

Visually, the two types of boxing appear the same to the average layman, except that sometimes the *internal* styles look too slow to be effective as self-defense systems. In reality, quite the opposite is true. In fact, muscular training as espoused by the *external* styles is restricted by age, whereas the spiritual development of the *internal* styles continues through life, actually becoming deeper and more profound with age. It is undeniable that often the use of a single part of the body in *external* boxing is admirable—but it requires much time and effort to perform it correctly, and the use of it often leaves other parts of the body open to attack. The strength of *internal* boxing, however, is hidden, and permeates everything in equal proportions. Stored within the body, the *ch'i* is virtually inexhaustible and can be gathered for use. Not being localized in any particular part of the body, the strength can suddenly shoot forth from any quarter.

In the practical application of the two styles, too, there are many other differences in terms of principles and methods. The *internal* styles are based upon *change*, upon the interplay of *yin* and *yang*, and upon how to win without resorting to violence. A master of an *internal* form can dodge, deflect, and counterattack instinctively, because his mental training has made him ready for anything.

An ancient boxing classic states: "Boxing is like taking a walk; striking an enemy is like snapping your fingers." This is not to belittle the power of the *external* forms. When an *external* master is in his prime, he is a veritable fighting machine. But machines break down with wear and tear and with age. The *internal* styles, in contrast, not only protect one through automatic self-defense mechanisms; they also bring health, and can be said, therefore, to teach both fighting and living skills at the same time.

CONCEPTS NEEDED FOR PRACTICE

A novice needs a strong desire to learn, confidence that he can eventually master the form, and the understanding to appreciate its function. He must be prepared both mentally and physically, and he must have the proper concept in mind. He is like a man setting off upon a journey—if he wants to reach his destination quickly and safely, he will choose the best transport and the shortest route. In the *internal* styles, however, the student is ultimately on a journey to discover himself.

The ideal student is one of middle age, since he has accumulated much knowledge and experience while growing. Confucius said: "A person at forty will not be diverted." This originally referred to ethical cultivation, but can be applied to any kind of learning. When young, a person tends to show off strength, but when he is older his strength will eventually fail him. Then he knows that what he had earlier was superficial and of no use to him. Guilt and regret then impel him to learn the art from the beginning. Now more quiet than when young, he turns to the spiritual aspect of the art and gains tranquility. To learn an *internal* art correctly, a student must do only one thing—*nothing* that is unnatural. (In Chinese, it is said that he must have *wu-wei*—the virtue of "doing nothing" that is not natural or spontaneous.) This ability to "do nothing" brings harmony to life, but takes a long time and great effort to achieve.

Wrong ideas can mislead the student—and they are rampant. Many divide the *internal* schools into *hard, soft,* and *change,* equating Hsing-i with *hard,* T'ai-chi with *soft,* and Pa-kua with *change.* On one level of discussion, this may be right; but when seen with a broader perspective this is far from correct. Others say that Hsing-i is for youngsters; Pa-kua, for the middle-aged; and T'ai-chi, for the old. How absurd! The three are actually joined together in a more intricate trinity—they are but three aspects of the same truth. From Hsing-i, you can learn the physical aspects of the *internal* function, while you can reach the spiritual essence of *internal boxing* from T'ai-chi and Pa-kua, providing that you study for years under a competent teacher, during which you work yourself to the limit of your ability.

All three of the *internal* martial arts are based on *i,* the will or the mind. The mind is the source of all action. The idea is to keep the mind still while the body moves. To remain still while the body moves in a linear fashion—that is Hsing-i; and to do so while the body moves in circles—that is Pa-kua. The idea is formed and the body moves in accord with the mind. *Hard* and *soft* are merely points of transition, extremes that are constantly in the process of turning into their opposites. Thus, it is wrong to say that one of these arts is *hard,* and another *soft.*

To learn the *internal* arts properly, then, the mind must dominate the body. At first, the student must adopt *wu-wei* and forget the self. Then he must go on to not only accept but even to embody these radical principles:

1. Boxing requires movement, but, first, the *internal* requires stillness;

2. To defeat an opponent requires strength, but, first, the *internal* requires softness;

3. Fighting requires speed, but, first, the *internal* requires slowness.

These basic three axioms comprise the best mode of transport for bringing the student quickly and easily to his goal. If he follows the principle of "To know first, to act second," rather than blindly going through the actions without any awareness of what he is doing, his achievement will be great.

NOTES ON PRACTICE

Beginners should be familiar with the standards of training as set down by the old masters. Training was and is the heart of the art. Knowledge cannot replace training, though it can improve the manner in which you train. When boxing and the other combative arts of China were at their zenith, men trained as though their lives depended on it. Many of them were convoy guards, and their lives did depend on the skills they honed over the years. Old masters insisted upon twenty years to learn the art of Pa-kua. The regimen of training often required six hours a day and included exhaustive solo forms, bag work, two-man exercises, and work with an arsenal of weapons. The study of martial skills required an athletic capacity now superseded by the invention of the gun.

Although the internal arts avoided feats of physical prowess, training in them was no less exhausting. It tested the nerve and the will of the student and left deep physical and psychological marks. But the skills forged over the years were absorbed into the person's nervous system, leaving no outward sign of extraordinary ability.

Nowadays, even with lower standards, training in internal boxing still requires at least one hour daily, six days a week. In this way, a degree of physical strength is maintained and mingled with a spirit of enquiry. With time, the two are fired by your growing commitment and produce a forged skill. In the first ten years of training, the beginner should do about twenty to thirty repetitions of the eight palm changes, in addition to the auxiliary exercises, on each day set aside for practice.

Practice should be done outside in natural surroundings, which encourage your body to acclimatize itself to natural conditions and help the mind to become calm. The best time for practice is around sunrise, when the air is fresh, the light penetrating, and the mind quiet. For relaxation and concentration, the area should be as private as possible. Observers distract and detract. Silence in a noisy world is rare, but it is also essential for sharpening and quieting your nerves; thus, pay attention to the postures and not to music or other things.

Begin practice gradually, and, as your body warms up, bend your legs more, take longer steps, and extend your arms. Once warmed up, speed should approximate brisk walking. If the movement is done too slowly, rhythm will not reveal itself; if too fast, the postures will lose clarity and crispness, creating confusion in the mind rather than relaxation. The rhythm should help to regulate the emotions. Speed is a result and not a goal—it comes only as a result of finely honed coordination and kinesiological economy.

Above all, the only way to prevent your postures from becoming mere mechanical performance is to keep your mind on your *tan-t'ien* and to relax unnecessary tension, thereby opening up your body, increasing your breathing capacity, and quickening the flow of *ch'i*. Through long practice, this leads to finely tuned synchronization of your muscular contractions (bodily movements) and in the end improves your mind.

An alternate form of learning the postures endorsed by the old masters is that of pausing several times in each posture while steadying the breath and the body. This allows the mind to focus on the body parts, to find and eliminate unnecessary tensions, and to sensitize the mind to the postural mistakes it must correct. The effects of gravity become more familiar as the mind comes to see more clearly how it relates to the body, and thus mechanical efficiency increases. The stress of static postures on the legs strengthens them and increases their flexibility and stamina. This also strengthens the tendons of the whole body from the toes to the fingertips. Some teachers advise counting the breaths for various periods of time, other simply pause for a moment. Breathe naturally, embracing the *ch'i* in the *tan-t'ien* while holding a posture.

Initially, the mind will rebel against holding the postures, and the muscles will ache, but, with repetition, the mind will adjust. For the mind to be still, first the body must be still. It is then that the sense of stillness comes. This teaches the student something of the discipline of the will and the value of silent stillness.

At the turn of the century, when leading boxers often worked as guards and were all-around combat experts, they used calisthenics and other forms of conditioning. The Taoists, however, emphasized the principle of naturalness in their internal arts that sought simplicity, eschewing artifice of any kind. At times, ancillary training is useful as a therapeutic tool, as swimming is for arthritis and calisthenics and weight training are for scoliosis. Though it may be a necessity, this type of therapeutic training will not develop the skill born of naturalness that the postures and training are designed to develop. "Auxiliary training," or training that is directed toward competitive ends and performance in public is unnecessary. Weight training, if organized around the postures and their principles, can be useful but is also unnecessary.

THE TEACHER-STUDENT RELATIONSHIP

Success in internal boxing often depends upon the relationship between the teacher and the student. Traditionally, this relationship was much like that of father and son. This aspect of the Chinese martial arts has not traveled well into commercial America, but a few words about this important relationship may help readers to understand an art decidedly different from the Hollywood nonsense seen in film, television, and the printed media.

The relationship between a student and his teacher derives from cultural mores based largely upon Confucian teachings on filial piety and family. Thus, in studying the internal arts, all the students of the same teacher regard themselves as brothers, with seniority based upon age and experience. They revere and respect the teacher and help him as needed in his daily life.

The intention of the teacher and the student must agree in order for the teaching to "take." This requires time and mutual trust. This trust must evolve out of respect and is reflected in mature self-restraint and behavior—and an occasional errand or gift. If a student's behavior is lacking, the teacher will abridge or withhold the teaching. Thus, transmission of the art requires not only respect but perseverance while respect is being worked out. The student at first acts out of courtesy but gradually comes to an attitude of genuinely caring for the teacher and following his guidance and doing whatever he can to help him. This earns the teaching. The technique, however, must be worked out through long, consistent training in which the teacher observes and disciplines the student's behavior, thus preventing the "right means from working in the wrong way"—that is, through teaching the art to the wrong person.

For his part, the superior teacher paces the teaching, giving the student what can be learned in a given period, praising effort and censuring idleness. He should welcome new students as adventures and not be afraid to stop teaching those too egocentric to learn. By and large, the relationship should make both parties more productive and happier—and, as Bertrand Russell once wrote, the Chinese prefer happiness to power (would that we could all be satisfied with that).

PART FOUR   Pa-kua Training

8

The Basics

Although Hsing-i is largely linear and fisted and Pa-kua circular and open-palmed, the philosophy and principles of one apply equally to the other. Both occupy moral bases established by Confucius and Lao-tzu. Teaching different doctrines, both men sought to produce a just man following a virtuous way—Confucius, through a macrocosmic social contract built on the family; Lao-tzu, through a societal perfection coming from a microcosmic individual effort to realize oneself. Confucius wanted to regulate society, while Lao-tzu sought to advise the individual. Confucius taught behavior, Lao-tzu taught correct breathing and hygiene.

And, like the other internal arts, Pa-kua teaches boxing as a discipline, not as an excuse to contend with others. The great master Teng Yun-feng once explained to a class in Peking that Pa-kua should be used to neutralize attacks but that the secret was *never to use it.* When a feisty student questioned, "Why, then, learn it?" Teng countered with, "If you don't want to learn it, get out of here." What he was saying is that while Pa-kua is permeated with self-defensive functions, one must avoid even the occasion of having to cause distress to another.

THE MAIN PRINCIPLES

Pa-kua is not an easy art to master. Although it can be learned in less time than the twenty years the old masters insisted upon, it does require regular and tedious practice over a period of several years. Chou Chi-ch'un, one of the leading modern historians of the Chinese martial arts, once said:

> Pa-kua is difficult to learn. You walk very slowly for two or three years, then go faster and, later, very fast. The chief aims are to move behind an opponent quickly and to strengthen the arms. Through the practice, heavy weights can later be attached to the arms without discomfort. At the turn of the century, a famous master went to Japan and, while there, supported the weight of a sumo wrestler on his outstretched arm! Often, accomplished boxers would carry a cup of tea in each palm while spinning and turning their bodies—all without spilling a single drop!

The most important principles of Pa-kua are:

1. *Move your body naturally.* The best rule to help you do this is to follow all the other rules. Avoid the rudimentary Shaolin and karate exercises, as they will only make you stiff and exhausted. The muscle building they encourage impedes the proper flow of *ch'i* in the body as well as its coordination and celerity of movement.

2. *Stretch your arm but withdraw your trapezius muscle.* (Although this may seem contradictory or antagonistic, it is an important part of Pa-kua. *See* "Internally Bound, Externally Stretched," below.) This strengthens the flow of *ch'i*. Another similar posture is to lower your waist by "holding" downward the small of the back muscles while also "feeling" the sacrum as if it were ready to spring up.

3. *Harmonize your vital energy and your strength.* Internal boxing insists that three things must be coordinated: the mind (*i*) must command, the strength (*li*) must obey, and the vital energy (*ch'i*) must follow. In the internal forms, *internal* truths must be transformed into

The Twelve Basic Principles

1. Clear your mind and keep your head erect and your neck straight. Look directly ahead.

2. Round your shoulders slightly, hollowing your chest and easing the movement of *ch'i*.

3. Turn your upper thighs slightly inward, protecting the lower navel so that the air can go deeply.

4. Breathe long and slowly through your nose.

5. To let your nerves function naturally, keep your body erect from the neck to the tip of your coccyx.

6. Relax your waist, tuck the tip of your coccyx in and upward, and slightly contract the sphincter muscle.

7. Sink your shoulders and drop your elbows. Only if your elbows hang can your shoulders sink, and only if your shoulders sink can *ch'i* go to your fingertips.

8. Touch your tongue to the roof of your mouth, close your mouth lightly, and let your teeth meet without pressure lest the *ch'i* be retarded. Then, exercise will produce saliva, which will irrigate the throat.

9. Pa-kua comes from the mind. It blends the external strength (*li*) and the internal energy (*ching*), thus enabling us to "seek stillness in movement."

10. Pa-kua walking is done, not with the legs straight, but with "sitting thighs," with the legs well bent. In walking, keep your feet low and "button" (*k'ou*—with your toes slightly inward) downward, causing your soles to cup the ground flatly as if walking in mud. When you walk, your front foot touches lightly, and when the rear foot is flat, it feels as if you are pushing down as in climbing a mountain. The ankle of your advancing foot brushes the other ankle as it passes. After a while your step will be as light and fast as running water.

11. Your waist is the big axis and is used to mobilize, stimulate, and move the four extremities. Before your body moves, your waist moves (Fig. 6).

12. In the basic palm, "Lotus-leaf Palm," keep your fingers separated and your palm concave. Your thumb is held horizontally, your index finger vertically, and your remaining fingers are proportionally bent so that your thumb, index finger, and little finger form a triangle.

external boxing forms, suggesting that thought and action must work in unison.

4. *Keep your* ch'i *concentrated in the* tan-t'ien *below the navel.* This psychic energy center (about three inches below the navel) should also mark your true center of gravity. To concentrate the vital energy there means to "sink" your strength from the upper to the lower torso in order to gain stability.

"INTERNALLY BOUND, EXTERNALLY STRETCHED"

Wang Shu-chin stressed the principle of *nei-kuo, wai-ch'eng* (internally bound, externally stretched), a maxim describing a kinesiological sense developed from long practice walking the circle (Fig. 3). "Internal binding" refers to the feeling produced by the muscles and connective tissue linking the upper torso to the area of the *tan-t'ien,* just below the

3. Wang Shu-chin Doing the "Squatting Tiger" of Pa-kua

navel, which corresponds also to the body's center of gravity. Surrounding this area and supporting its organs are the muscular sheathing of the abdomen, the omentum of the intestines, the *quadratus lumborum*, and the anchoring tendons of the diaphragm, which stretch upward from the lumbar spine to the costal margin forming a dome over the viscera. This network of muscles and supporting tissue produces a tugging sensation around the *tan-t'ien* as though it were a bag being pulled slightly by connecting fibers. The tugging or bound/wrapped sensation is not produced by over-articulation so much as by simply doing and feeling the postures.

"External stretching" is evident in the antagonistic articulation of the hand, wrist, and elbow. When extended, the arms stretch the tendons by keeping the shoulders and elbows down. The scapulae do not slide forward and the chest is not contracted but held naturally. The breath is directed mentally down to the navel, and up through the diaphragm and lungs. Correct breathing feels as if the whole torso is inflating like a bellows. Inflating the lungs expands the ribs coincident with the downward pull of the diaphragm, which presses on the intestines and the *tan-t'ien* area, producing the feeling in the torso of "internally bound, externally stretched." (Fig. 4).

The deep breathing, antagonistically extended arms, upright torso, and low center of gravity (achieved by bending the legs) combine with the kinesthetics of moving on a double circle (circling with yourself as pivot, and turning around an external circle), swinging, rolling, and spinning, to provide the holistic and very real feel of this dynamic and pervasive principle. Stated simply, the internal binding (or sinking) counterbalances the energy you direct through your arms outward toward the center of the circle. Functionally, this adds to your root and prevents an opponent from countering your external energy. Meditationally, it sinks, nourishes, and maintains your *ch'i*, your mind, and your *tan-t'ien* (Figs. 5, 6).

4. Author Smith Punching Wang Shu-chin (1960)

5. Wang Shu-chin Doing the "Hawk" of Pa-kua

6. Wang Shu-chin Doing the "Monkey" of Pa-kua

THE NINE PALACES

The idea of "Nine Palaces" is both practical and esoteric. It derives from ancient Taoist cosmology and dance. Originally, it signified nine stations or portals that adepts would dance among, sealing off this dimension from evil outside influences. Nine is an auspicious number to Asians, and among the Cabalists is regarded as the number of powers under God. In Chinese boxing, the number nine is used in the names of boxing styles as diverse as Little Nine-Heaven Boxing (*Hsiao Chiu T'ien Ch'uan*) and Cheng Man-ch'ing's version of Yang-style T'ai-chi, in which emphasis is put on opening the nine joints or parts of the body (the top of the head, the neck, the wrists, the elbows, the shoulders, the hips, the sacrum, the knees, and the ankles), and in which the development of one's skill passes through nine phases.

The cosmic dance found its way into Pa-kua boxing as a practical means to develop footwork fluency while extending the exercise from a single circle to a figure-8 (Fig. 7) to a nine-station regimen (Fig. 8).

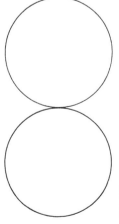

7. The Pa-kua Figure-8

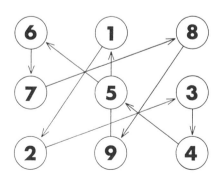

8. The Pa-kua Nine Stations

The nine palaces also portray the $3 \times 3 = 9$ relativity of the body divided into three corresponding sets of bases, centers, and tips:

1. The upper body has the shoulders as the base, the elbows as the center, and the hands as the tip.
2. The lower body has the hips as the base, the knees as the center, and the feet as the tip.
3. The whole body has the *tan-t'ien* (seat of power) as the base, the heart (seat of emotion) as the center, and the head (seat of intelligence) as the tip.

	Base	*Center*	*Tip*
Upper body	Shoulders	Elbows	Hands
Lower body	Hips	Knees	Feet
Whole body	*Tan-t'ien*	Heart	Head

In Pa-kua, the sets are further tactically divided into the high, middle, and low techniques. The head is the high or "heavenly" tip penetrating the skies. The spirit rises and the essences can combine harmoniously in one place. The torso is the middle set: if it stays erect and does not lean, the nervous system can respond quickly and the *ch'i* can flow easily. The feet are the low or "earthly" base, so important for stability and agility. The student must distinguish three sections: the head is the tip; the torso, the center; and the feet, the base—the head must be sure; the body, well rooted; and the feet, fluent. If any are awry, the mind (*i*) cannot function properly. All is one. Pa-kua's power comes from all components of the body coordinating with the mind and with the *ch'i*. This coming together is the meaning of the old phrase, "The Nine Palaces return to one."

Sun Lu-t'ang, in his *Pa-kua ch'uan hsueh* [A Study of Pa-kua Boxing; Peking, 1916], touches on the esoteric aspect of the Nine Palaces as follows (paraphrased):

> The Nine Palaces are a cosmological arrangement and are not unique to Pa-kua boxing. They are found in *Chi Men Ch'uan* (Mysterious Gate Boxing), which also has movements around nine stations.... The Nine Palaces are the points of integration whereby the prebirth (*hsien-t'ien*) and the postbirth (*hou-t'ien*) energies [those you are born with and those you develop] unite. The purpose of the Nine Palaces is to enable the student to obey the divine will (*i*). When the Nine Palaces are integrated, you are ready for the final stage, the "great awakening."
>
> The Nine Palaces are realized best when the upper/lower and inner/outer aspects of a student are harmonized. As the years pass, his whole being is reformed. His sinews and membranes change continuously, coming under more direct control of his brain. In turn, his brain then is controlled by his spirit, and, ultimately, by the divine mind, or the *tao*.
>
> As this process occurs, the student occasionally will glimpse his original or divine face for a moment. This moment must recur many times for him to be able to progress to the final phase, in which he can will the divine face to reappear. Therefore, one who trains at Pa-kua diligently for a considerable amount of time displays his nature at its best.

Do not be concerned if the subject of what Sun spoke of seems too esoteric or abstruse. It is not important that you understand every idea—especially at the beginning. Merely do the practice as set forth in Part Two, and, over time, your body will help your mind to come to an understanding.

OTHER PRINCIPLES

Kuo Feng-ch'ih once said that it is easy for a weak person or one who knows nothing of boxing at all to learn Pa-kua. Such a person is not preoccupied with past instruction and does not resist the advice given but merely goes ahead and follows it. Boxing masters advise that three requirements must be followed in learning Pa-kua:

1. You should remain *relaxed*. If you are tense, your mind can neither think calmly nor react quickly. If your body is tense, your motions will be sluggish and you will be slow to respond. With relaxation your mind will be liberated and your body will attain a happy, unencumbered circulation of air and blood.

2. You should heed the *slow*, a word that refers not only to action but also to a state of mind free from impatience and anxiety. Slowness harmonizes outside and inside influences. By beginning slowly, you as a novice will have sufficient time *to seek, listen to, feel for,* and *apprehend* the essence of Pa-kua and for your body to adjust itself, various muscles reforming themselves in line with your practice. Gradually, the action will become faster, but your internal focus will remain as slow and as steady as when you did it slowly.

3. You should strive for *evenness* of actions and breathing. Pa-kua will prevent erratic and unbalanced movements by teaching you to sink your breath to your *tan-t'ien*, which will permit normal breathing even when you are moving strenuously. Practice itself will harmonize action and breathing. You adjust your breathing unconsciously in time to slow or fast movement, just as we unconsciously adjust our breathing while eating. Pa-kua, like eating, is natural, and regulates the breath in the same way. It stresses naturalness; teachers often tell their students to observe children and to breathe naturally as they do.

4. Keep your chest relaxed, not held out in a military fashion, to help the circulation of your *ch'i*. Hold your tongue so that the tip

touches the hard palate (the roof of the mouth) and hold your head straight (as though a string from the ceiling were attached to the center of your head). Expand or round your back by dropping your shoulders; drop your elbows, too, when extending your arms.

5. Master the techniques of:

Rise (*ch'i*)—start to raise your right hand;

Drill (*tsuan*)—as it ascends, turn the palm upward in a clockwise drilling strike;

Fall (*lo*)—begin to lower your hand, palm still up;

Overturn (*fan*)—as it descends, twist the right palm downward in a counterclockwise strike or grasp.

9

Walking the Circle

THE CONCEPT OF THE CIRCLE

The essence of Pa-kua is to be found in the circling movement and in its changes. The practice is based upon "walking the circle," which means that you should walk around an imaginary or a marked circle and periodically change direction.

Everything in nature tends to be circular: the sun, the moon, the cycles of the seasons. And a baby's smile. Even straight lines are only shorter segments of a bigger circle. The underlying Taoist principles with the palm changes correlated to the eight *kua* in an endless circle provide an exercise of the whole person in managing his body in peace or struggle. As you walk the circle, the exercise becomes a link to psycho-physiological processes that increase your knowledge of yourself. This knowledge then results in apperception of the relationship between the macrocosm and the microcosm; thus Pa-kua ends by blending meditation and self-defense, an exercise in handling reality.

Pa-kua reflects the universe: the universe turns; the weather rolls; we walk. When you walk around the circle, you walk the universe and your inscape at the same time. Your thoughts derive from the universe, and they expand until thought and action become one. Perceive and know your mind, for it directs thought like a canal directs water. And when you know your mind and its adaptations to circumstances, you can direct it. The person who can handle the rigor

9. Author Smith, Walking the Pa-kua Circle

and continuous change of Pa-kua can live with the ambiguities of life: he has gained the intelligence of the art.

Walking the circle is the chief exercise in Pa-kua. You walk the circle for a few minutes or hours, your body erect, legs well bent, *ch'i* at the *tan-t'ien,* and your arms exerting "internally bound, externally stretched'' energy (Fig. 9). Periodically, you change hands and body, holding the same posture while you circle in the opposite direction.

Begin with a circle six to twelve feet in diameter, and as you progress, reduce it, commensurate with your skill. Initially walk with your knees slightly bent, and as your body warms up bend them more. The lowest height and most difficult position puts you in a sitting posture—it is said that the old-timers practiced in a room with only a five-foot ceiling—but the middle height we use here is the most useful. It develops leg strength without sacrificing mobility and develops the knee muscles and ligaments—a prerequisite for the lowest walking.

To maximize the effect of circle walking, experiment with several steps. You may begin by suspending your rear foot and pausing at the front ankle to develop stability. Or you may walk by touching the rear foot down forward in a ''false'' step and then making the step slightly longer before transferring your weight onto the foot. Finally, using the separation principle of Tai-chi, you may step forward, putting your entire sole on the floor before weighting it. This is difficult and must be done slowly and in a low posture for best results. Practicing long and short steps is also encouraged, so that you may better analyze uses. Also, lifting the knees high in walking develops kicking skills while resting the lower back. At first, speed can be an impediment. It is better to integrate the basics at a slow or moderate pace before adding speed.

The circle itself can be changed in various ways beyond the simple clockwise and counterclockwise. After walking circles of varying sizes, accustoming your legs to the regimen, and practicing the changes, increase the complexity by walking a figure-8 (Fig. 7), linking the two circles at the intersection. When this is mastered, walk through each of nine stations, circling each (Fig. 8). Go in both directions and arbitrarily use whatever posture you wish, but always feel the presence of an opponent. This will add variety to your Pa-kua.

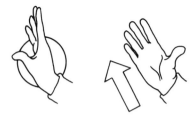

1. STANDING   2. CARRYING   3. SUPPORTING   4. CUTTING

THE EIGHT MAJOR PALM SHAPES

Force in Pa-kua is transmitted to the target in circular movements through the legs, body, and hands using the body weight and rooting. The body is an avenue that must be kept clear, through which the mind directs the *ch'i*. The final impact is enhanced by articulating the palms into eight major shapes (Fig. 10). Often, one shape will lead into or follow another in a response sequence.

1. STANDING PALM exemplifies the Pa-kua maxim "internally bound, externally stretched." The hand, wrist, and elbow all have this strength. This palm is used in the basic walking posture around the circle. Excellent for strengthening the tendons of the arms as well as the spine, it may be articulated as a deflection, a push to the body, or a "blinder" slap or as a strike to the head or chin. Wang called this hand style, in which the thumb and little finger form a triangle, the "Lotus-leaf Palm."

2. CARRYING PALM can be used as a chop to vital points, or as a push upward or directly ahead. It may also be used as a combined deflection-attack, as in the T'ai-chi postures called FAIR LADY WORKS AT SHUTTLES, and also is part of the Pa-kua form named WHITE SNAKE STICKS OUT TONGUE, in which one hand serves as a block while the other strikes simultaneously beneath it.

3. SUPPORTING PALM is a pushing or spearing strike depending on whether or not the fingers are held pointing straight out or downward. It is fused into most of the change patterns as a sequential movement (for example, in WHITE MONKEY

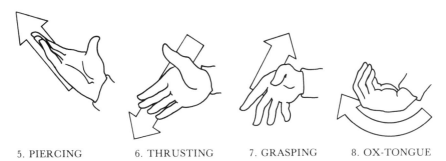

| 5. PIERCING | 6. THRUSTING | 7. GRASPING | 8. OX-TONGUE |

10. The Eight Major Palm Shapes

PRESENTS A PEACH, you may use SUPPORTING PALMS to push the opponent's lower abdomen before lifting the hands up into PIERCING PALMS). It may also be employed as an upholding deflection and will balance the centrifugal force of your body when moving and turning.

4. CUTTING PALM is a lateral chop with a scraping action. It combines the hand edge with pressing forward and can be articulated into a clamp. A major tactic of Pa-kua, it is seen in the initial chop in the SQUATTING TIGER form of the SINGLE CHANGE OF PALM.

5. PIERCING PALM penetrates with the fingers in a drilling or screwing action. It is seen in SINGLE CHANGE OF PALM, in which, after chopping, you may turn your palm to pierce with your fingers. It is also used to attack the opponent's external obliques or to jostle him on a vertical axis.

6. THRUSTING PALM is a vertical chopping downward seen especially in GIANT ROC SPREADS WINGS, but it may also be used as a deflection.

7. GRASPING PALM corresponds to the WARD OFF of T'ai-chi. It is used to grasp the opponent's wrist, elbow, shoulder, throat, belt, or leg. The retracting hand is invariably GRASPING PALM. Articulated, it can be held palm in or out. It is seen in the swing back out of SINGLE CHANGE OF PALM, after the first PIERCING of DOUBLE CHANGE OF PALM, and in the first high deflection of HAWK SOARS UP TO HEAVEN.

8. OX-TONGUE PALM corresponds to the T'ai-chi posture called SINGLE WHIP; it is used to poke with the fingers or to strike/ deflect with the back of the wrist.

THE EIGHT CHANGES

1. SINGLE CHANGE OF PALM (*Tan Huan Chang*)
Start by standing erect, feet held with toes 45° apart, heels together and left foot facing straight ahead, on the circumference of the circle (Fig. 11). Raise your arms outward, palms down (Fig. 12), and, as they come up to shoulder level, turn your palms up (Fig. 13). Continuing, raise your hands overhead till they face (Fig. 14). Now shift most of your weight to your right foot, turn your upper torso leftward, your left palm pressing out, your right palm pressing down (Fig. 15). Shifting the rest of your weight to your right foot, put your left foot down on the circle ahead as your left and right palms continue pressing outward and down, respectively (Fig. 16). Stay erect, sinking the shoulders, elbows, and body.

Walk with your left hand focused on the center of the circle. Your feet are so close that your ankles brush in passing, the advancing foot touching down heel first. Begin each change by bringing your outside foot forward and toeing it in (usually) or out (only in YELLOW DRAGON ROLLS OVER). To change here, bring your right foot forward and toe it in ahead of your left without changing your palms (Fig. 17). Shift your weight to your right foot and turn your waist leftward while your left foot pivots on the ball (Fig. 18). Now step forward with your left foot, your left hand CUTTING forward while your right hand GRASPS, palm up, and retracts to your right side (Fig. 19). This posture is 60% rear-weighted and is called SQUATTING TIGER.

Now toe-out and transfer your weight to your left foot as you suspend your right foot near your left ankle and PIERCE your left armpit with your right hand, palm up, "embracing" your left shoulder, your body twisting slightly leftward (Fig. 20). As you turn rightward back toward the center, your right hand goes from under your left arm and slightly upward, while your left hand turns over, palm up, near your

11   12   13

14   15   16

17   18   19

20

21

22

23

right elbow and both arms swing back rightward (Fig. 21). As your
right palm continues its turn toward the center, extend your right leg,
the toes down, and sit, sinking squarely down on your pelvis (Fig. 22).
For those familiar with T'ai-chi, on this swing you protect by present-
ing two WARD OFFS—with the arm and the leg—to the center. In
Wang's system, the knee is brought higher than in others. Put your
foot down on the circle and walk, your right palm turning gradually
with your torso to the center and your left palm pressing down (Fig.
23).

24

2. DOUBLE CHANGE OF PALM (*Shuang Huan Chang*)

Walking the circle with your left palm focused on the center (Fig. 24), toe-in your right foot and begin as in SINGLE CHANGE (Figs. 25, 26), pausing at SQUATTING TIGER (Fig. 27). Toe-out your left foot, depress with your left palm, and step forward with your right foot, PIERCING your right hand, palm up, over your depressing left palm (Figs. 28, 29).

Now toe-in your right foot, turn your waist leftward, and take your right hand high, your palm down, "folding" (Fig. 30). Simultane-

25

26

27

28

29

30

31

32

ously, move your left hand, palm up, near your left waist, shift your weight to your right foot, and suspend your left foot at your right ankle (Fig. 31). Step backward with your left foot, pivoting on your right heel, and squat, scraping your left hand, palm up, down your left leg toward your ankle (Fig. 32). Drop your right hand, palm down, near your left elbow.

Next, toe-out your left foot slightly and shift your weight onto it. At the same time, turn your left hand over and press the palm edge for-

33

34

ward in CUTTING as you rise, your right hand following your left elbow (Fig. 33). Transfer all your weight to your left foot, PIERCING with your right palm upward under your left armpit and suspending your right foot at your left ankle (Fig. 34). Swinging rightward toward the center, raise your right knee high, extending your right palm forward and pressing your left palm down (Fig. 35), and continue to walk the circle (Fig. 36), gradually turning your torso and hands toward the center.

35

36

37 38 39

40 41

3. HAWK SOARS UP TO HEAVEN (*Yao Fei Li T'ien*)

This change is also called UP-AND-DOWN CHANGE PALMS (*Shang-hsia huan chang*). Walking with your left hand focused on the center (Fig. 37), toe-in your right foot deeply (Fig. 38). Then toe-out your left foot in a short step leftward and raise your left hand high with the palm out in GRASPING (Fig. 39). Step forward and toe-in your right foot, your back toward the center, and SPEAR your right hand, palm in, over your left, palm down, at your right elbow (Fig. 40). This right spear can use either the CARRYING or the GRASPING palm.

Next, pivot on your right heel leftward and suspend your left foot at your right ankle (Fig. 41). Then step backward to the circle with your left foot, squatting on your right leg, and CUT with both of your palms. Your right hand is higher than your left, which is aligned with

42

43

44

45

your left leg, and you are 85% rear-weighted (Fig. 42). Toe-out your left foot as in DOUBLE CHANGE OF PALM, rise, and shift your weight to it, CUTTING forward with your left palm edge while holding your right hand, palm up, at your right hip (Fig. 43).

Finally, do SINGLE CHANGE OF PALM as before, PIERCING with your right palm under your left armpit, turning leftward, and suspending your right foot at your left ankle (Fig. 44). Swing rightward, separating your hands, carrying your right knee high (Fig. 45), and, as your right palm stretches toward the center, put your right foot down (Fig. 46). Then continue to walk the circle, gradually turning your torso and hands toward the center.

46

47

48

4.   YELLOW DRAGON ROLLS OVER (*Huang Lung Fan Shen*)

DRAGON is the only change in which you toe-out with your outside
foot as it comes forward instead of toeing-in as usual. Walking with
your left palm focused on the center (Fig. 47), make an extreme toe-
out with your right foot (Fig. 48) and shift your weight onto it until
your left foot comes up on its toes. Then step forward with your left
foot parallel to your right in a HORSE STANCE. Your back is now to

49   50   51

52   53

the center, your left palm forward at ear level, and your right hand, palm down, near your navel (Fig. 49). Shift your weight to your left foot and suspend your right foot at your left knee, extending your left hand, palm edge CUTTING forward, at eyebrow level, your right hand at your left armpit, as you lean forward (Fig. 50). Finally, twist your body slightly leftward, taking your right hand, palm up, under your left armpit (Fig. 51), then swing rightward, raising your knee, your right palm out as before, in SINGLE CHANGE OF PALM (Figs. 52, 53). Then walk the circle, gradually turning your torso and hands toward the center.

54   55   56

57   58

5. WHITE SNAKE STICKS OUT TONGUE (*Pai She T'u Shen*)

Walking with your left hand toward the center of the circle (Fig. 54), toe-in your right foot (Fig. 55). Swing your bent left arm down and to the right with your waist (Fig. 56). As you shift your weight onto your right foot, take your left hand, palm out, and move it in a large counterclockwise circle overhead (Fig. 57), turning your waist leftward, and ending with your left hand palm up and at chin level, in PIERCING palm, and your right hand palm up, in GRASPING palm, near your right hip (Fig. 58). Most of your weight is on your right foot; your left is placed so that only the ball of the foot touches the ground.

Take a half-step forward with your left foot, while your left hand, palm up, PIERCES, your weight 60% rear-loaded (Fig. 59). Toe-out your left foot, press your left palm down, and step forward with your

59

60   61   62

63   64

right foot while PIERCING with your right hand, palm up, over your
depressing left palm (Figs. 60, 61). Your weight is again 60% rear-
weighted. Now shift your weight to your left foot, toe-in your right
foot, and raise your right hand high, palm down, GRASPING, while
bringing your left hand, palm up, near your left hip (Fig. 62).

Now shift your weight to your right foot and suspend your left foot
at your right ankle. Pivoting on your right heel, bring your right palm
near your ear (Fig. 63). Move your left hand and your left foot

65

66

67

backward in SNAKE step, turn to face front, and separate your arms,
your left palm deflecting high in CARRYING palm and your right palm
pushing forward, SUPPORTING, as in the T'ai-chi posture FAIR LADY
WORKS AT SHUTTLES. Your weight is 70% front-loaded (Fig. 64).
Finally, shift all your weight forward to your left leg and do SINGLE
CHANGE OF PALM as before, swinging out of it rightward, putting
your right foot down ahead, and walk, gradually turning your torso
and hands toward the center (Figs. 65, 66, 67).

68

69

70

6. GIANT ROC SPREADS WINGS (*Ta P'eng Chan Ch'ih*)
Walking with your left hand toward the center (Fig. 68), toe-in your
right foot and turn your waist rightward, shifting your weight to your
right foot, your left forearm turning in across your body (Fig. 69). As
your waist begins to turn leftward, move your left arm in a clockwise
circle down, pivoting at the elbow (Fig. 70). Step to your left and forward with your left foot and circle your left hand, palm out and CUT-
TING upward, while retracting your right hand, palm up, to your right
hip (Fig. 71). Step forward with your right foot, toed-in, and make an
OX-TONGUE palm with your right hand at your right hip (Fig. 72).

71

72   73   74

75

76

77

78

Next, lift your left foot, toes down, knee high, as your left arm starts to sweep overhead (Fig. 73). Pivot to the left on your right heel and continue circling your left arm in GRASPING palm (Fig. 74) while you unclasp your right hook and circle it upward from the rear (Fig. 75). Now place your left foot down back on the circle in a 60% rear-weighted posture, simultaneously chopping with your right palm, and end by THRUSTING downward, slapping your palms en route. Your left palm protects the right side of your head—that side toward the center—and your right palm stops at waist level (Fig. 76).

As you shift your weight to your left foot, suspend your right foot at your left ankle and drop your left hand, palm up, on your right forearm, which has also been turned upward (Fig. 77). Step forward with your right foot and begin to walk (Fig. 78). As you walk, extend your crossed arms high and forward, separating them to each side in

79

80

81

82

PHOENIX, walking style, your left STANDING palm, slightly higher than your right (Figs. 79–82). Figures 79–82 show arm movement from a static posture, to differentiate the arm movement for the reader. Actually, the arms only move—opening and extending—as you walk.

83

84

85

7. WHITE MONKEY PRESENTS A PEACH (*Pai Yuan Hsien T'ao*)
Walking with your left palm toward the center (Fig. 83), toe-in your
right foot deeply (Fig. 84). Turn your waist leftward, and, as it continues and your weight shifts onto your right foot, pivot your left foot
on its ball and open your arms (Fig. 85). Step forward with your left

86   87   88

89   90

foot to the circle (Fig. 86), and, as you shift your weight forward to it, raise your right leg, the knee high, and bring both palms upward as though carrying a tray with PIERCING palms (Fig. 87). Step out with your right foot and gradually turn your torso and hands toward the center as you walk (Figs. 88–90).

91   92   93

94   95   96

8. WHIRLWIND PALMS (*Hsuan Feng Chang*)

This change, which blends the palms, is also called EIGHT IMMOR-
TALS CROSS THE SEA (*Pa Hsien Kuo Hai*). Walking with your left
hand focused on the center (Fig. 91), toe-in your right foot in a wide
stance, dropping both arms as you turn your waist rightward (Fig. 92).
Step toward the center with your left foot, circling your left hand from
the elbow in a backhanded motion PIERCING downward, and retract
your right hand, palm up, in GRASPING palm, at your right hip (Figs.
93, 94). Toe-out your left foot, and, while pressing down your left
palm, step forward a full step with your right foot (Fig. 95). Put your
right foot down toed-in slightly, and, as your weight shifts onto your
right foot, turn your body sideward, your waist leading the action, and
PIERCE with your right palm over your depressing left SUPPORTING
palm (Fig. 96).

97 98

99 100

101 102

103

Now circle your left palm clockwise down and out to the side, palm up, but don't change your right palm (Fig. 97). Pivoting on your right heel, raise your left arm, palm down, over the right arm, which circles underneath, palm up (Fig. 98). Step back with your left foot in line with your right heel, into a HORSE stance, and shift your weight to it, turning your torso leftward while your arms remain in an "embrace" posture (Figs. 99, 100). As your weight begins to shift to your right foot, drop your hands, palms down, in a circle (Fig. 101). Continue shifting your weight to your right foot, taking your hands, palms in, upward in a counterclockwise circle (Fig. 102). Now shift your weight to your left foot and turn your waist leftward, carrying both CUTTING palms in, across your body (Fig. 103).

Still in the HORSE stance, and with most of your weight on your left foot, drop your left hand, palm up, near your right elbow and extend

104

105

106

107

108

your right hand forward, palm down (Fig. 104). Swing your right hand rightward, CUTTING laterally, your left palm following your right elbow, and your weight going to your right foot, your left foot suspended at your right ankle (Fig. 105).

Next, step forward, toeing out your left foot, and extend your right hand, GRASPING, palm out, overhead while PIERCING with your left hand, palm up, down and forward in the BALL-HOLDING posture (Fig. 106). Toe-in your right foot as you turn leftward, without changing your arms (Fig. 107). Shift your weight to your right foot while extending your right hand, palm up, to the side, circling your left hand, palm up, and suspending your left foot near your right knee (Fig. 108).

109   110   111

112   113

Pivoting on your right heel, bring your left arm over the descending right arm in an "embrace" posture, palms facing (Fig. 109). Completing the pivot on your right heel, put your left foot down in a 60% rear-weighted stance, CUTTING laterally with your left palm edge. Your right hand, palm up, follows your left elbow (Fig. 110). Do SINGLE CHANGE OF PALM and walk the circle with your right palm focused on the center (Figs. 111–113).

114

115 116

To close the exercise, walk with your right hand extended toward the center of circle. Toe-in your left foot (Fig. 114) and then toe-out your right foot until your feet are parallel, dropping your hands, your right on top, as you turn rightward (Fig. 115). Continue dropping your hands past your sides (Fig. 116) and bring them up and outward

117   118   119

120   121   122

overhead, palms down (Fig. 117). As you begin to press downward (Fig. 118), turn your waist rightward (Fig. 119) and leftward (Fig. 120), then rightward and leftward once more, then back to the center (Fig. 121) and stand (Fig. 122).

123

124

125

Alternatively, you may do Chen P'an-ling's shorter close. On the last step of walking with your right hand extended toward the center, bring your left (rear) foot up so that the heels almost touch, and then lower both hands, palms facing up below your navel, keeping both knees bent (Fig. 123). Raise both arms out to the sides and overhead, palms facing, and stand up and inhale (Fig. 124). Lower both hands, moving palms down the center of your body to your *tan-t'ien*. Bend you knees and exhale (Fig. 125).

Conclusion

The popularity of Hsing-i and Pa-kua in China was greatly increased through the skill and the many publications of the famous Sun Lu-t'ang, whose *Ch'uan-i Shu Cheng* [The Real Explanation of Boxing (1929)] and *Pa-kua Ch'uan Hsueh* [A Study of Pa-kua Boxing (1916)] were written to present the true aspects of the art. We have used some of the information contained in his books in giving the introduction to the art and in talking about Pa-kua and Hsing-i masters. It is only natural, therefore, that we end this presentation with his own words.

> The Tao permeates the universe and is the origin of both *yin* and *yang*. In boxing, the Tao is symbolized by the internal arts of Hsing-i, Pa-kua, and T'ai-chi. Although these three arts are different, they are based upon the same principle: everything begins, is, and ends in emptiness. One's original energy (*yuan ch'i*) must be maintained. This is the power that keeps the sky blue and that makes the earth calm; it is also the source of achievement in man. . . . Confucius said: "From the greatest sincerity comes the greatest achievement."

Diligent practice in the internal arts is, then, a discipline born out of sincerity, a system of self-control over conduct that leads to achievement. The word discipline itself comes from the Latin roots (*dis* + *capere*, to hold apart) meaning both a system of education and a method of training that employs rigorous control—thus, a leading forth of your true self through self-control. Although fully Chinese in their conception and aesthetics, the three internal martial arts of Hsing-i, Pa-kua, and T'ai-chi are also excellent expressions of what the ancient Greeks called *araté* (fr. Gr. *areskein*, to please; akin to *arariskein*, to fit)—a noble ideal that Plato called "the holistic striving for excellence in terms of beauty, strength, and wisdom." As in *araté*, excellence in the internal arts is only possible while one is striving. Those who think they have attained excellence have already lost it, bypassing *aidos* (modesty) for hubris, or overbearing pride. Therefore, in order to best perfect your Pa-kua and Hsing-i skills, always work hard and remain humble.

Finally, description is no substitute for practice. As Master Li Kuei-yuan once wrote: "Rules are taught by the teachers, but the essence can only be comprehended by the boxer himself." And the essence can only be obtained through practice. Put simply, as you practice you obtain the essence.

Index

Gentle principle, 93
GIANT ROC SPREADS WINGS, 93, 131, 150–154
GRAPSING PALM, 131
Great Ultimate, 91

Han Ch'i-ying, 97
Hangchou, 5
hard and soft, as merely points of transition, 104
HAWK SOARS UP TO HEAVEN, 92, 131, 141–143
heart, 92, 93
Heaven, 89, 92
Heng ch'uan, 22, 37–38
hexagrams, 90
Hochien Hsien, 98
"holding" downward the small of the back, 114
Honan, 5, 8
Hopei Province, 8, 94, 96, 98
horizontal strength, 101
HORSE POSTURE (Pa-kua), 144, 159
HORSE STYLE (Hsing-i), 47, 63–65
Hou hsing, 58–62
hou-t'ien, 123
Hsiao Chiu T'ien Ch'uan, 121
Hsiao Hai-po, 98
hsien-t'ien, 123
hsin, 17
Hsing-i: basic posture of, 20 (*see also* san-t'i); becomes a part of your life, 4; as boxing with the mind, 9; and Buddhist/Taoist practices, 6, 11; as cooperative, 6; and dedication, 5; history of, 7–8; as an internal art, 3; as largely linear, 113; and

muscles/ligaments, 9; as natural as a baby's movements, 22; and Pa-kua, 94, 101, 104; and sin-gle/double weighting, 10–11; as training the mind even more than it does the body, 5; as unique, 4; used only in the greatest extremity, 4
hsing-i ch'uan, 3
hsu, 4
Hsuan Feng Chang, 157
Huang Lung Fan Shen, 144
Hu hsing, 55–57
Hu k'ou, 16–17
hubris, 88

i, 104, 114, 122
I Ching, 89
I-hsien, 96
INFINITY POSTURE, 23, 24, 40, 41, 45
inguinal crease, 24
"internal bidding," 116–118
internal energy, 115.
    See also ch'i
internal fighting systems, as differ-ent from the Shaolin, 3
internal martial arts, 101
internal system (*nei-chia*), 89
internal truths, as transformed into external boxing forms, 114–116
"Internally bound, externally stretched," 116–118, 128–129, 130
intrinsic energy, 4, 9
"Invincible Cobra Ch'eng," 96

Japan, Wang's school in, 100
Japanese martial arts, 5

the hidden Taoist ranks, 96; essence of, 92, 127, 168; and Hsing-I, as complementary, 3, 4–5, 11, 18, 94; main principles of, 113–116; masters of, 93–101; as never to be used, 113; origin of, as unknown, 93; philosophy and practice of, 89–93; popularity of, in China, 167; as requiring twenty years to master, 105; and Sun Lu-t'ang, 167; transmission of force in, 130; Wang Shu-chin's method of, 98, 100, 135

Pa-kua chang, 89

Pa-kua Ch'uan Hseuh, 123, 167

Pa-kua Lien-huan Chang, 98

Pa-kua Linked Palm, 98

P'ao ch'uan, 22, 35–36

Pao-ting, 97

Pausing several times in each posture, as a training technique, 107

"pecking hand," 75, 77

Peking, 94

Peng ch'uan, 22, 30, 31

PHOENIX, 80

Physiological and esoteric princples, 11

P'i ch'uan, 22, 26–29

PIERCING PALM, 131

Plato, 87–88

Postbirth energy, 123

POUNDING FIST, 22, 35–36, 41, 43

Practice: best time for, 106; as harmonizing action and breathing, 124; and pausing in each posture, 107; and slowness, 124; and speed, 106

Prebirth energy, 12, 123

Psychic energy center, 116. *See also* tan-t'ien

quiet attentiveness, 4

Real Explanation of Boxing, The, 97, 167

Receptive principle, 92

relationship between the teacher and the student, 108–109

Relaxed state, importance of, 124

Rise, 18, 125

Russell, Bertrand, 109

san-t'i, as basic Hsing-i posture, 24–25; in passim, in descriptions of the movements

San-ts'eng t'ao-li, 4

scissor-step, 50, 51, 52, 53

seed-essence, 4

self-improvement, 3–4

Sha Hui-tsu, 95

Shang Tao-yuan, 94

Shang Yun-hsiang, 8

Shanghai, 5

Shang-hisa huan chang, 141

Shansi, 7, 8

Shantung, 93

Shaolin, 3

She hsing, 78–79

shen, 4

Shih Liu, 96

Shuang Huan Chang, 136

SINGLE CHANGE OF PALM, 92, 131, 132–135, 136, 142, 145, 162

single circle, 121

SINGLE WHIP, 75, 131

Six Coordinations, 15–16

sixty-four hexagrams, evolved from the combinations of the eight trigrams, 91

vertical strength, 101
virtue of "doing nothing," 103–104
visible energy, 11
vital spirit, 4

walking the circle, 110, 127–165
Wan Lai-sheng, 96
Wang Hsiang, 8, 93
Wang Hsiang-chai, 98
Wang Li-te, 97
Wang Shu-chin: 7n, 8, 22, 92, 98, 101, 116, 130, 135; and school in Japan, 100
WARD OFF, 131, 135
WATER STRIDER STYLE, 47, 66–68
Western boxing and karate cannot help, 5
WHIRLWIND PALMS, 93, 157–165
WHITE MONKEY PRESENTS A PEACH, 93, 130–131, 155–156

WHITE SNAKE STICKS OUT TONGUE, 93, 130, 146–149
will, or mind, 104, 113, 122
wu chi, 23
wu hsing, 21, 22
wu-wei, 103, 104

yang, 11, 89, 90, 91, 102
Yang-style T'ai-chi, 121
Yao Fei Li T'ien, 141
Yao hsing, 72–73
YELLOW DRAGON ROLLS OVER, 92, 132, 144–145
Yen hsing, 74–77
yin, 11, 89, 90, 91, 102
yin and yang, 11, 167
Ying-Hsiung hsing, 82–86
yuan ch'i, 167
Yuan Tao, 22
Yueh Fei, 7
Yun shou, 66

OTHER TITLES IN THE
TUTTLE MARTIAL ARTS LIBRARY

THE ART OF WAR

The Definitive Interpretation of Sun Tzu's Classic Book of Strategy
By Stephen F. Kaufman
5 ¼ x 8 ½, 128 pp., paperback, $12.95
ISBN-10: 0-8048-3080-0
ISBN-13: 978-0-8048-3080-5

Sun Tzu's classic text, translated by Steven Kaufman, is perhaps the best-known and most highly regarded treatise on strategy ever written. Although its wisdom is over two thousand years old, its principles are timeless for today's boardroom battle-fields.

THE ART OF SHAOLIN KUNG FU

The Secrets of Kung Fu for Self-Defense, Health, and Enlightenment
By Wong Kiew Kit
6 x 9 ¼, 240 pp., paperback, $15.95
ISBN-10: 0-8048-3439-3
ISBN-13: 978-0-8048-3439-1

A complete and comprehensive introduction to kung fu and other aspects of ancient Shaolin wisdom, this text shows how kung fu can bring you health, vitality, mental focus, and spiritual joy.

JEET KUNE DO BASICS

By David Cheng
6 ¾ x 9 ¾, 192 pp., paperback, $12.95
ISBN-10: 0-8048-3542-X
ISBN-13: 978-0-8048-3542-8

A useful and informative book offering a detailed overview of Jeet Kune Do, its history, basic elements, and some beginning fighting techniques. Also included is information on schools, finding teachers, and a comprehensive list of resources.

THE SECRETS OF EAGLE CLAW KUNG FU
Ying Jow Pai
By Leung Shum and Jeanne Chin
6 x 9, 240 pp., paperback, $19.95
ISBN-10: 0-8048-3215-3
ISBN-13: 978-0-8048-3215-1

Eagle Claw kung fu is one of the few modern Chinese martial arts derived from actual military combat experience. This text contains information on its essential secrets and insider tips, along with detailed explanations of the fundamentals of Eagle Claw kung fu.

THE SWORD POLISHER'S RECORD
The Way of Kung Fu
By Adam Hsu
5 ½ x 8 ½, 208 pp., paperback, $16.95
ISBN-10: 0-8048-3138-6
ISBN-13: 978-0-8048-3138-3

A collection of essays about the art of kung fu, highlighted with over seventy photographs and drawings. Each section examines a different aspect of kung fu, including its foundations and principles, the future of kung fu, and, most importantly, its place in the martial arts.

KUNGFU BASICS
By Paul Eng
6 ¾ x 9 ¾, 192 pp., paperback, $12.95
ISBN-10: 0-8048-3494-6
ISBN-13: 978-0-8048-3494-0

The continuing rise in popularity of kungfu is well served by a basic guide. This book teaches the beginning student patterns and sets, the training of internal force, and strategies for victory, along with highlighting the basic elements of style.

OTHER TITLES IN THE TUTTLE MARTIAL ARTS LIBRARY

POLICE KUNG FU
The Personal Combat Handbook of the Taiwan National Police
By Man Kam Lo
6 x 9, 136 pp., paperback, $16.95
ISBN-10: 0-8048-3271-4
ISBN-13: 978-0-8048-3271-7

A comprehensive approach for the use of traditional kung fu by law enforcement personal, this text shows how to maximize personal safety while minimizing the necessary use of force.

COMPLETE WING CHUN
The Definitive Guide to Wing Chun's History and Traditions
By Robert Chu, Rene Ritchie, and Y. Wu
6 x 9, 160 pp., paperback, $16.95
ISBN-10: 0-8048-3141-6
ISBN-13: 978-0-8048-3141-3

This definitive text presents seldom seen information on a dozen branches of the Wing Chun art, and offers readers a side-by-side comparison by outlining each system in terms of history, principles, basics, and training methods.

SHAOLIN LOHAN KUNG-FU
By P'ng Chye Khim and Donn F. Draeger
6 x 9, 172 pp., paperback, $14.95
ISBN-10: 0-8048-1698-0
ISBN-13: 978-0-8048-1698-4

Lohan Kung-Fu is a Chinese fighting technique developed in the Shaolin Temple by the Indian monk Bodhidharma. Intended as a supplement to actual training, this book gives the history of the Shaolin arts and then continues with a detailed explanation of the Lohan form.